Illicit Trade

Misuse of Containerized Maritime Shipping in the Global Trade of Counterfeits

This document, as well as any data and map included herein, are without prejudice to the status of or sovereignty over any territory, to the delimitation of international frontiers and boundaries and to the name of any territory, city or area.

Please cite this publication as:
OECD/EUIPO (2021), *Misuse of Containerized Maritime Shipping in the Global Trade of Counterfeits*, Illicit Trade, OECD Publishing, Paris, *https://doi.org/10.1787/e39d8939-en*.

ISBN 978-92-64-32008-6 (print)
ISBN 978-92-64-64738-1 (pdf)
ISBN 978-92-64-43808-8 (HTML)
ISBN 978-92-64-49828-0 (epub)

Illicit Trade
ISSN 2617-5827 (print)
ISSN 2617-5835 (online)

European Union Intellectual Property Office
ISBN 978-92-72-42444-2 (print)
ISBN 978-92-72-42443-5 (pdf)
Catalogue number OA-05-21-007-EN-C (print)
Catalogue number OA-05-21-007-EN-N (pdf)

Photo credits: Cover ©Shutterstock/Avigator Fortuner.

Corrigenda to publications may be found on line at: *www.oecd.org/about/publishing/corrigenda.htm*.

© OECD/European Union Intellectual Property Office 2021

The use of this work, whether digital or print, is governed by the Terms and Conditions to be found at *http://www.oecd.org/termsandconditions*.

Preface

Illicit trade in counterfeit and pirated goods damages economic growth and can harm individual and collective health and safety; fuels corruption; undermines sound public governance, the rule of law and citizens' trust in government; and can ultimately threaten political stability. The COVID-19 pandemic has accelerated illicit trade, alarming law enforcement in many parts of the world.

To deal with this risk in an effective way, we need more information on its scale, scope and impact. This is precisely the purpose of this joint study by the OECD and the EUIPO, which sheds new light on the misuse of containerised maritime transport for trade in fake goods.

We are very pleased that our two organisations were able to co-operate to develop this solid and unique evidence-based research. We are confident that the results will facilitate the development of innovative policy options to respond to the challenges of trade that misuses containerised maritime transport fake goods, and consequently to promote clean trade in the post-COVID recovery.

Christian Archambeau,
Executive Director,
EUIPO

Elsa Pilichowski,
Director,
OECD, Public Governance Directorate

Foreword

Illicit trade in fake goods is a significant and growing threat in a globalised and innovation-driven economy, undermining good governance, the rule of law and citizens' trust in government. It not only has a negative impact on the sales and profits of affected firms and on the economy in general, but also poses major health and safety threats to consumers.

To provide policy makers with solid empirical evidence about this threat, the OECD and the EU Intellectual Property Office (EUIPO) joined forces to carry out a series of analytical studies that deepen our understanding of the scale and magnitude of the problem. The results have been published in a set of reports starting with *Trade in Counterfeit and Pirated Goods: Mapping the Economic Impact* (2016), and including the most recent ones *Trends in Trade in Counterfeit and Pirated Goods* (2019), and *Illicit Trade in Counterfeit Pharmaceuticals* (2020).

The results are worrying. Trade in counterfeit and pirated goods amounted to up to 3.3 % of world trade in 2016; when considering only imports into the EU, fake goods amounted to up to 6.8 % of imports. Counterfeiters operate swiftly in the globalised economy, misusing modern logistical solutions and legitimate trade facilitation mechanisms and thrive in economies lacking good governance standards.

Evidence shows that, while criminals continue to use all available modes of transport for illicit trade, seizures from commercial maritime container shipping continue to dominate in terms of volume and value of goods seized. The COVID-19 pandemic has intensified the problem: criminal networks have reacted very quickly to the crisis and adapted their strategies to take advantage of the shifting landscape.

This study provides a detailed analysis of economy- and industry-specific patterns in the misuse of containerised maritime transport by counterfeiters. Such information is crucially needed, not only for better understanding this threat, but also for developing effective governance responses to support post-COVID recovery.

This study was carried out under the auspices of the OECD's Task Force on Countering Illicit Trade, which focuses on evidence-based research and advanced analytics to assist policy makers in mapping and understanding the vulnerabilities exploited and created by illicit trade.

This document was approved by the Public Governance Committee via written procedure on 31st December 2020 and prepared for publication by the OECD Secretariat.

Acknowledgements

This report was prepared by the OECD Public Governance Directorate together with the European Union Intellectual Property Office (EUIPO).

At the OECD this study was conducted under the Task Force on Countering Illicit Trade (TF-CIT). The study was shared with other OECD committees with relevant expertise in the area of trade, health policy and innovation.

The report was prepared by Piotr Stryszowski, Senior Economist and Florence Mouradian, Economist at the OECD Directorate for Public Governance jointly with Michał Kazimierczak, Economist at the European Observatory on Infringements of Intellectual Property Rights of the EUIPO and Nathan Wajsman, Chief Economist, EUIPO. Peter Avery, Senior Economist, provided significant inputs. The authors wish to thank the OECD experts who provided valuable knowledge and insights: Morgane Gaudiau and Stéphane Jacobzone from the OECD Public Governance Directorate, Evdokia Moïse and Silvia Sorescu from the OECD Trade Directorate, and Olaf Merk from the International Transport Forum.

The authors would also like to thank experts from the OECD member countries and participants of several seminars and workshops for their valuable assistance. Special expressions of appreciation are given to Riikka Pakkanen from Finnish Customs, George Agius from Malta Customs as well as to Massimo Antonelli, Siegmar Reiss and Laurent Szymkowiak from the EUIPO.

Raquel Paramo and Andrea Uhrhammer provided editorial and production support.

The database on customs seizures was provided by the World Customs Organization (WCO) and supplemented with regional data submitted by the European Commission's Directorate-General for Taxation and Customs Union, the US Customs and Border Protection Agency and the US Immigration and Customs Enforcement. The authors express their gratitude for the data and for the valuable support of these institutions.

Table of contents

Preface 3

Foreword 4

Acknowledgements 5

Executive summary 9

1 Introduction 11
    References 12

2 Containerships – the engines of globalization and trade 13
    Containers – multimodal revolution 14
    The backbone of globalization 14
    Industry structure 18
    Market developments 20
    The effects of containerization 20
    The industry in 2020 (COVID-19) 23
    References 25

3 Containerships: legal frameworks and threats of illicit trade 27
    Hague-Visby Rules 27
    Bill of Lading (BOL) 28
    Rotterdam Rules 28
    Multimodal containers – legal settings 29
    Legal frameworks to counter illicit trade in maritime transport 29
    References 36

4 Containerships and global trade in fake products – the Evidence 37
    Where do we source our information? 37
    Trade in counterfeits in container ships -- overall picture 39
    Key maritime routes for illicit trade 59
    References 68

5 Conclusions and areas for action 69
    Next steps 70

Annex A. 71
  Notes 76

Tables

Table 2.1. Seaborne trade in 2018	13
Table 2.2. Container trade in 2000 and 2018, by economy (Millions of TEUs)	15
Table 2.3. World container throughput, by region, 2018 (Millions of TEUs)	16
Table 2.4. World's largest container ports in 2018, and their size in 1990, (Millions of TEUs)	16
Table 2.5. Liner shipping connectivity index in 2006 and 2019[1]	17
Table 2.6. Top 20 container companies, as of 7 July 2020	19
Table 2.7. World seaborne trade, 2013-19, (Millions of tonnes)	20
Table 4.1. Key producers and transit points in illicit trade in fakes in containerships, in five main targeted industries (2016)	45
Table 4.2. Main ports of exportation of fakes from provenance economies (2016)	62
Table 4.3. Main countries of entry of containers in maritime transport from the five major counterfeit provenance countries (2016)	63
Table 4.4. Main ports of entry of containers from the five major counterfeit provenance countries (2016)	64
Table 4.5. Selected acquisitions of port operation undertakings by Chinese firms in Europe	66
Table 4.6. Selected acquisitions of port operation undertakings by Chinese firms in Asia	67
Table 4.7. Selected acquisition of port operation undertakings by Chinese firms in other regions	67
Table A A.1. Main countries of entry of containers in maritime transport from China (2016)	71
Table A A.2. Main ports of entry of containers in maritime transport from China (2016)	71
Table A A.3. Main countries of entry of containers in maritime transport from Turkey (2016)	72
Table A A.4. Main ports of entry of containers in maritime transport from Turkey (2016)	72
Table A A.5. Main countries of entry of containers in maritime transport from Singapore (2016)	73
Table A A.6. Main ports of entry of containers in maritime transport from Singapore (2016)	73
Table A A.7. Main countries of entry of containers in maritime transport from Hong Kong (China) (2016)	74
Table A A.8. Main ports of entry of containers in maritime transport from Hong Kong (China) (2016)	74
Table A A.9. Main countries of entry of containers in maritime transport from United Arab Emirates (2016)	75
Table A A.10. Main ports of entry of containers in maritime transport from United Arab Emirates (2016)	75

Figures

Figure 2.1 The volume of containers (thousand of TEUs) handled in the European Union ports between 2005 and 2018	18
Figure 2.2. Containerised ocean freight rates developments per week in selected trade lanes	24
Figure 4.1. Conveyance methods for counterfeit and pirated products, 2014-16	40
Figure 4.2. Value of exports of fakes against the value of maritime port infrastructure investment by provenance economy. 2016	40
Figure 4.3. Value of exports of fakes against the value of maritime containers transport (weight) by provenance economy. 2016.	41
Figure 4.4. Value of counterfeits seized by transports modes across selected IP-intense product categories, 2014-16	42
Figure 4.5. Top 10 provenance economies in the value seized maritime containers transporting counterfeits, 2014-16	42
Figure 4.6. Economies most likely to use containers for exporting fake goods among the top 20 provenance economies in terms of their propensity to export counterfeit goods (GTRIC-e, average 2014-16)	43
Figure 4.7. Share of the value of fake exports by transport mode for the top 20 provenance economies of fake goods in terms of GTRIC-e (average 2014-16)	44
Figure 4.8. Shipment methods for seized counterfeit perfumes and cosmetics, 2014-2016	46
Figure 4.9. Provenance economies of seized containers containing perfumes and cosmetics, 2014-16	46
Figure 4.10. Counterfeit perfumes and cosmetics: quantity of total exports by containers against total value of seizures of fake goods, 2016	47

Figure 4.11. Counterfeit perfumes and cosmetics: quantity of legal exports by containers against value of seizures of fake goods by containers, 2016 — 48
Figure 4.12. Shipment methods for seized counterfeit articles of leather and handbags, 2011-13 — 49
Figure 4.13. Top provenance economies of sea shipments containing counterfeit leather articles and handbags, 2014-16 — 49
Figure 4.14. Counterfeit leather articles and handbags: quantity of legal exports by containers against total value of seizures of fake goods, 2016 — 50
Figure 4.15. Counterfeit leather articles and handbags: quantity of legal exports by containers against value of seizures of fake goods by containers, 2016 — 51
Figure 4.16. Shipment methods for seized counterfeit clothing and textile fabrics, 2011-13 — 52
Figure 4.17. Provenance economies of seized containers containing counterfeit clothes, 2014-16 — 52
Figure 4.18. Counterfeit clothing: quantity of legal exports by containers against total value of seizures of fake goods, 2016 — 53
Figure 4.19. Counterfeit clothing: quantity of legal exports by containers against value of seizures of fake goods by containers, 2016 — 53
Figure 4.20. Shipment methods for seized counterfeit electronics and electrical equipment, 2014-16 — 54
Figure 4.21. Provenance economies of containers containing counterfeit electronics and electrical equipment, 2014-16 — 55
Figure 4.22. Counterfeit electronics and electrical goods: quantity of legal exports by containers against total value of seizures of fake goods, 2016 — 55
Figure 4.23. Counterfeit electronics and electrical equipment; quantity of legal exports by containers against value of seizures of fake goods by containers, 2016 — 56
Figure 4.24. Shipment methods for seized counterfeit toys and games, 2014-16 — 57
Figure 4.25. Counterfeit toys and games: quantity of legal exports by containers against total value of seizures of fake goods, 2016 — 58
Figure 4.26. Counterfeit toys and games: quantity of legal exports by containers against total value of seizures of fake goods by containers, 2016 — 58
Figure 4.27. Correlation between the Port LSCI index and proxy for trade in counterfeits. Economy-level, 2016 — 60
Figure 4.28. Correlation between the Bilateral LSCI index and a proxy for trade in counterfeits. Economy-level, 2016 — 60
Figure 4.29. Correlation between the Container port traffic index and a proxy for trade in counterfeits. Economy-level, 2016 — 61

Boxes

Box 2.1. Counterfeit trade deception techniques — 21
Box 3.1. Electronic BOL — 28
Box 4.1. The OECD database on seized counterfeit and pirated products — 38
Box 4.2. Belt and Road Initiative (BRI) — 65

Follow OECD Publications on:

 http://twitter.com/OECD_Pubs

 http://www.facebook.com/OECDPublications

 http://www.linkedin.com/groups/OECD-Publications-4645871

 http://www.youtube.com/oecdilibrary

http://www.oecd.org/oecddirect/

Executive summary

Trade in counterfeit goods represents a longstanding, and growing, worldwide socio-economic risk that threatens effective public governance, efficient business and the well-being of consumers. At the same time, it is becoming a major source of income for organised criminal groups. It also damages economic growth by undermining both business's revenue and their incentive to innovate.

Counterfeit and pirated products tend to be shipped by virtually every means of transport. In terms of number of seizures, trafficking of fakes via small parcels is growing and becoming a significant problem in terms of enforcement; however, in terms of value, counterfeits transported by container ship clearly dominate.

Over the past decades, containers have become the universal means to aggregate goods into standardised, uniform cargo. The introduction of containers was a revolutionary change for transport that offered new logistical possibilities, boosted efficiency and greatly reduced the overall cost of international trade. At the same time, smugglers found it appealing, given the ease and low risk of stowing not only counterfeit products, but also narcotics and other types of contraband, and even undocumented migrants in the containers.

Available data confirm the high intensity of misuse of containerised maritime transport by counterfeiters. The analysis in this report uses two sorts of data. The first is information on trade in counterfeit goods, which is based on customs data regarding seizures of counterfeit goods obtained from the World Customs Organization, the European Commission's Directorate-General for Taxation and Customs Union and from the US Customs and Border Protection Agency (CBP). The second includes data on trade with container ships from the OECD International Transport Forum (ITF) database, Eurostat Comext, and indices on containerised maritime transport developed by UNCTAD (United Nations Conference of Trade and Development).

A review of the data showed that, while the highest number of customs seizures of counterfeit and pirated products were from postal parcels, sea transport accounted for the most seized value. In 2016, containerships carried 56% of the total value of seized counterfeits.

The highest number of counterfeit shipments originated in South East Asia, including China and Hong Kong (China), India, Malaysia, Thailand and Singapore; while Mexico, Turkey and the United Arab Emirates also remain among the top provenance economies for counterfeit and pirated goods traded worldwide during the considered period.

Additional analysis carried out for the European Union showed that over half of containers transported in 2016 by ships from economies known to be major sources of counterfeits entered the EU through Germany, the Netherlands and United Kingdom. There are also some EU countries, such as Bulgaria, Croatia, Greece and Romania, with relatively low volumes of containers trade in general, but with a high level of imports from counterfeiting-intense economies.

Ongoing and planned infrastructure developments in the EU could significantly change the patterns of imports of fake goods through containers. The Chinese Belt and Road Initiative is of particular relevance in this context, as it could result in a substantial growth of fakes entering the European Union in container ships through ports in the Mediterranean region.

To combat illicit trade, a number of risk-assessment and targeting methods have been adapted for containerised shipping, in particular to target illicit trade in narcotics and hazardous and prohibited goods. However, it appears that the illicit trade in counterfeits has not been a high priority for customs, as shipments of counterfeits are commonly perceived as "commercial trade infractions" rather than criminal activity. Consequently, existing enforcement efforts may not be adequately tailored to respond to this risk.

Some efforts have been made by the industry to enhance co-ordination to counter the threat of illicit trade in maritime transport. A good example is the "declaration of intent", in which well-known brand owners, vessel operators and freight forwarders worked together to develop voluntary guidelines to raise awareness of the importance of gathering sufficient information on the parties using their shipping services. It appears that there is considerable scope for improvement in this regard.

1 Introduction

Illicit trade in counterfeit and pirated goods[1] is a growing and significant problem. Globalisation opens up new opportunities for criminal networks to expand the scope and scale of their operations in illicit trade in such goods. These issues need to be addressed, as trade in fakes is a significant risk that undermines good governance, the rule of law and citizens' trust in government, and can ultimately threaten political stability.

In order to improve the factual understanding of counterfeit and pirated trade and provide evidence for policymakers to formulate policies, the OECD and the European Union Intellectual Property Office (EUIPO) together carried out a series of comprehensive economic assessments of the problem. Their latest study has found that imports of counterfeit and pirated goods amounted to up to USD 509 billion in 2016, or around 3.3% of global trade (OECD/EUIPO, 2019).

The studies have explored how counterfeiters operate, showing that the decision of a party to engage in the illegal production of counterfeit or pirated goods involves determinations of: i) what products will be counterfeited or pirated; ii) where the products will be produced; iii) where the infringement will take place; iv) what geographic markets will be targeted; and v) how products will be shipped to end markets without being intercepted.

Regarding transport modes (point v), the process of transporting and distributing products internationally involves a number of business entities, including transport operators. The operators include small parcel shippers such as express courier companies and postal services, rail and truck carriers, air cargo companies and seaborne vessels (including containerships) (ICC, 2015). Transport operators are essential in supporting international trade, playing a major role in the supply chain and the transportation of genuine goods, and, counterfeits (ICC, 2015).

The OECD/EUIPO work has provided empirical evidence and identified the policy gaps related to the misuse of small parcels, shipped either by postal or courier services, in the global trade of fake goods (OECD/EUIPO, 2018b). This new report complements the research in this area by providing empirical evidence about the misuse of container ships in trade in counterfeits, and about the governance and economic drivers as well as policy gaps that enable them.

As noted in previous OECD/EUIPO studies, a high percentage of the global value of trade in genuine goods is conducted via seaborne vessels. However, the United Nations Office on Drugs and Crime (UNODC) also noted that less than 2% of this amount is inspected (UNODC, 2018). This results in significant opportunities for criminal networks to abuse this critical supply chain channel, at low risk. Counterfeiters have been quick to exploit opportunities in this regard. According to an OECD/EUIPO (2019) report, only 10% of the number of seizures made by customs authorities worldwide between 2014 and 2016 concerned sea/vessels, but they carried 56% of the total value of the seizures.

To combat the illicit trade, a number of risk-assessment and targeting methods have been adapted for containerized shipping, and customs administrations have robust policies in place to target illicit containerized trade of narcotics, hazardous and prohibited goods. However, it appears that the illicit trade in counterfeits has not been a high priority for customs as shipments of counterfeits are commonly perceived as "commercial trade infractions" rather than criminal activity.

Consequently, existing enforcement efforts may not be tailored adequately to respond to counterfeiting. Customs may not check for counterfeits with the same scrutiny as other illicit goods. Freight forwarders, carriers and shipping companies may also not have the right systems in place to implement anti-piracy policies to identify exporters and importers of fakes. Due to the relatively low-priority given to gathering intelligence and information on counterfeit shipping methods, counterfeits remain "low risk and high reward" for opportunistic criminal networks. The second part of the analysis will focus on policies for action aim to address these gaps.

The following tailored qualitative and quantitative analyses aim to deepen understanding of the drivers and motives of counterfeiters and pirates to misuse maritime transport to facilitate their illicit operations. The quantitative part establishes links between the intensity of trade in counterfeit goods via container ships from a given economy (origin and transit) and indicators on the quality of the maritime infrastructure, logistic facilities, and relevant economic and governance measures for the ports concerned.

References

ICC/BASCAP (2015), *Roles And Responsibilities Of Intermediaries: Fighting Counterfeiting And Piracy In The Supply Chain*, International Chamber of Commerce's (ICC) Business Action to Stop Counterfeiting and Piracy (BASCAP) https://iccwbo.org/content/uploads/sites/3/2015/03/ICC-BASCAP-Roles-and-Responsibilities-of-Intermediaries.pdf

OECD/EUIPO (2019), *Trends in Trade in Counterfeit and Pirated Goods*, Illicit Trade, OECD Publishing, Paris, https://doi.org/10.1787/g2g9f533-en.

OECD/EUIPO (2018b), *Misuse of Small Parcels for Trade in Counterfeit Goods: Facts and Trends*, OECD Publishing, Paris, https://doi.org/10.1787/9789264307858-en.

UNODC (2018), https://www.unodc.org/ropan/en/BorderControl/container-control/ccp.html

2 Containerships – the engines of globalization and trade

Seaborne transport plays an important role in world trade, accounting for more than 80% of the volume of merchandise traded between countries, and more than 70% of the total value of trade (UNCTAD, 2019).[2] In 2018, world merchandise trade[3] grew by 3.0 per cent, just above the 2.9 per cent increase in world GDP over the same period. It totaled some USD 19.7 trillion (WTO, 2019), more than USD 13.8 trillion of which is estimated to have been shipped by sea, in one of five basic types of vessels (UNCTAD, 2019 and Rushton, Croucher and Baker, 2017):

- Oil tankers, which are designed to carry large volumes of crude oil;
- Dry bulk carriers, which are designed to carry loose, dry commodities such as iron ore, coal and grain;
- General cargo ships, which are multi-purpose vessels designed to carry general cargo, including roll-on-roll-off vessels that are commonly used to transport vehicles;
- Container ships, which are designed to carry standard shipping containers that are capable of transporting a wide range of products;
- Other ships, which include specialized tankers designed to transport liquified oil and natural gases and parcel (chemical) tankers.

In terms of weight, the principal products transported by sea are bulk commodities, which tend to have relatively low weight unit values, such as iron ore, coal, crude oil and grain (Table 1). Higher value container freight, while accounting for about 16% of total tonnage, is estimated to account for about 60% of the total value of seaborne trade, or more than USD 8 trillion in 2018 (Scerra, 2020).

Table 2.1. Seaborne trade in 2018

Item	Volume (Millions of tonnes)	Percent of total
Minor bulk	2,028	17.2
Crude oil	1,992	16.8
Containers	1,875	15.8
Iron ore	1,455	12.3
Coal	1,292	10.9
Oil products	1,023	8.6
Grain	477	4.0
Gas	461	3.9
Chemicals	325	2.7
Other dry cargo	928	12.3

Source: Clarksons Research, 2020.

Containers – multimodal revolution

This report focuses on container ships, which have evolved in recent decades to become a powerful, cost effective, efficient means for moving a vast range of non-bulk commodities internationally. Other types of seaborne vessels seem to have little potential for carrying counterfeit products.

Before containerization, goods were usually handled manually as break bulk cargo. Typically, goods would be loaded onto a vehicle from the factory and taken to a port warehouse where they would be offloaded and stored awaiting the next vessel. When the vessel arrived, they would be moved to the side of the ship along with other cargo to be lowered or carried into the hold and packed by dockworkers. The ship might call at several other ports before off-loading a given consignment of cargo. Each port visit would slow the delivery of other cargo. Delivered cargo might then have been offloaded into another warehouse before being picked up and delivered to its destination. Multiple handling and delays made transport costly, time consuming and unreliable.

Over the decades, efforts focused on the creation of a standard shipping system that could speed up the processes and introduce time and costs efficiencies. Notable improvements include development in 1952 of the Transporter into the CONtainer EXpress or CONEX box system by the US Army. In 1955, a twist lock mechanism was introduced atop each of the four corners of a container. This mechanism allowed the container to be easily secured, piled in stacks, and lifted using cranes.

During the first 20 years of containerization, many container sizes and corner fittings were used. Consequently, there were numerous incompatible container systems. The standards that refer to sizes and fitting have evolved out of a series of discussion among main international shipping, railroad and trucking companies in Europe and the US. The standards were formalized in a set of ISO (International Organization for Standardization) recommendations, published in late 1960s and early 1970s. Specifically ISO standard 668 defines the dimensions, R-790 establishes identification markings, R-1161 relates to corner fittings and R-1897 defines minimum internal dimensions of containers. In addition, each container is allocated a standardized ISO 6346 reporting mark (ownership code), that is issued by the International Container Bureau (Bureau International des Containers B.I.C.).

Today, there are still many types and a number of standardized sizes, but a vast majority of the containers in global trade are "general purpose" containers, made of durable steel, designed to be carried on ships, rail or trucks. Container capacity is expressed in twenty-foot equivalent units (TEU). One TEU represents containerized cargo capacity equal to one standard 20-foot container.[4] Over time, the size of containers has grown; port operators indicate that most cargo is now shipped in 40-foot containers.

In the process, containers have become the universal means to ship a vast array of goods. This cargo can be easily handled, transported using various modes, and stored. Introduction of containers was in fact a revolutionary change for transport that offered new logistical possibilities, boosted efficiency and greatly reduced the overall cost of international trade (Levinson, 2016). Ironically, the technique was initially thought to represent a minor innovation, which was not suitable for moving most types of cargo, and not practical for long-haul international shipments from North America to Asia and Europe.

The backbone of globalization

Over time, the innovation revolutionized international trade, driving improvements in handling, storage and distribution techniques. Dedicated container ports have been developed worldwide, providing a platform for economies to enhance global operations. During the 2000-2018 period alone, container trade rose by more than three-fold, from 224.8 to 792.7 million TEUs, led by China's impressive growth (Table 2.2). On a regional basis, Asia accounted for almost two-thirds of container trade in 2018, followed distantly by Europe and North America (Table 2.3). The rise in container trade has been supported by marked growth in the size of dedicated ports: the largest in 1990 handled 5.2 million TEUs of cargo; in 2018, six ports handled more than 20 million TEUs, led by Shanghai's 42.0 million TEUs (Table 2.4).

Table 2.2. Container trade in 2000 and 2018, by economy (Millions of TEUs)

Economy	2000	2018	Percent change	Share of world total (Percent)	
				2000	2018
China	41.0	225.8	450.8	18.2	28.5
United States	28.3	54.7	93.2	12.6	6.9
Singapore	17.1	36.6	114.0	7.6	4.6
Korea	9.0	28.9	220.5	4.0	3.7
Malaysia	4.6	25.0	437.6	2.1	3.1
Japan	13.1	22.4	71.3	5.8	2.8
Hong Kong, China	22.6[1]	19.6	(13.1)	10.1	2.5
Germany	7.7	19.6	154.7	3.4	2.5
United Arab Emirates	5.1	19.1	276.9	2.2	2.4
Spain	5.8	17.2	196.9	2.6	2.2
India	2.5	16.4	568.5	1.1	2.1
Viet Nam	1.2	16.4	1,276.2	0.5	2.1
Netherlands	6.4	14.8	131.4	2.9	1.9
Indonesia	3.8	12.9	238.4	1.7	1.6
Belgium	5.1	12.7	150.8	2.3	1.6
United Kingdom	6.4	11.7	81.8	2.9	1.5
Thailand	3.2	11.2	251.9	1.4	1.4
Italy	6.9	10.5	52.4	3.1	1.3
Brazil	2.4	10.3	327.4	1.1	1.3
Turkey	1.6	9.9	524.7	0.7	1.3
Australia	3.5	8.7	146.9	1.6	1.1
Saudi Arabia	1.5	8.7	476.9	0.7	1.1
Philippines	3.0	8.6	184.9	1.3	1.1
Sri Lanka	1.7	7.0	304.0	0.8	0.9
Mexico	1.3	7.0	430.5	0.6	0.9
Panama	2.4	6.9	190.0	1.1	0.9
Canada	2.9	6.7	127.6	1.3	0.8
France	2.9	6.4	117.9	1.3	0.8
Russian Federation	0.3	6.3	1,903.1	0.1	0.8
Egypt	1.6	6.2	278.4	0.7	0.8
Other	9.7	124.5	1,179.4	4.3	15.7
World	224.8	792.7	252.6	100.0	100.0

1 Data are for 2005.
Note: Aggregated container port traffic by economy.
Source: World Bank, 2020.

Table 2.3. World container throughput, by region, 2018 (Millions of TEUs)

Region	Volume of trade	Percent of total
Asia	510.5	64.4
Europe	125.9	15.9
North America	61.4	7.7
Latin America and Caribbean	51.7	6.5
Africa	30.9	3.9
Oceana	12.9	1.6
World total	793.3	100.0

Source: UNCTAD, 2019.

Table 2.4. World's largest container ports in 2018, and their size in 1990, (Millions of TEUs)

Port	Economy	1990	2018
Shanghai	China	0.5	42.0
Singapore	Singapore	5.2	36.6
Ningbo-Zhoushan	China	0.0	26.4
Shenzhen	China	0.0	25.7
Guangzhou	China	0.1	21.9
Busan	Korea	2.3	21.7
Hong Kong	Hong Kong, China	5.1	19.6
Qingdao	China	0.1	19.3
Tianjin	China	0.3	16.0
Jebel Ali	United Arab Emirates	1.1	15.0
Rotterdam	Netherlands	3.7	14.5
Port Klang	Malaysia	0.5	12.3
Antwerp	Belgium	1.6	11.1
Xiamen	China	0.0	10.7
Kaohsiung	Chinese Taipei	3.5	10.5
Dalian	China	0.0	9.8
Los Angeles	United States	2.6	9.5
Tanjung Pelepas	Malaysia	0.0	9.0
Hamburg	Germany	2.0	8.8
Keihin ports	Japan	1.5	8.1
Long Beach	United States	(1)	8.1
Laem Chabang	Thailand	(1)	8.1
Tanjung Priok	Indonesia	(1)	7.8
New York and New Jersey	United States	(1)	7.2
Colombo	Sri Lanka	(1)	7.1

1 Not available.
Sources: Journal of Commerce Staff, 2019 and Levinson, 2016.

In addition to the above indicators, the relative importance of countries in maritime container transport can be examined using a liner connectivity index development by UNCTAD (presented in the next table).

The index shows that China enhanced its leadership in connectivity during 2006-20, with its index rising by 52% during this period (Table 2.5). Singapore, Korea and Malaysia also strengthened their positions significantly, rising to the second, third and four positions, respectively, as the United States and several European countries slipped in the overall ranking.

Table 2.5. Liner shipping connectivity index in 2006 and 2019[1]

Economy	2006	2019	Percent change
China	100	152	52
Singapore	80	108	35
Korea	68	105	54
Malaysia	65	94	45
United States	83	90	9
Hong Kong, China	84	89	7
Belgium	76	88	16
Netherlands	73	88	21
United Kingdom	79	85	7
Spain	70	84	20
Germany	77	83	7
Chinese Taipei	60	79	31
Italy	60	73	20
France	58	73	25
United Arab Emirates	49	71	46
Japan	75	71	-6
Egypt	47	67	43
Viet Nam	21	67	213
Saudi Arabia	41	63	53
Sri Lanka	34	62	83
Greece	33	61	86
Morocco	12	58	383
Turkey	31	57	88
India	41	56	36
Thailand	38	53	40

1 The index uses China, the most connected country, as the basis for comparison, setting its 2006 performance at 100.
Source: UNCTAD, 2020.

Ports in the EU have also reported strong growth rates over the past years. Except for the brief period related to financial crisis. European ports registered steady growth exceeding 50% over this period. Figure 2.1 illustrates the raising volume of containers handled in the European Union ports between 2005 and 2018.

Figure 2.1 The volume of containers (thousand of TEUs) handled in the European Union ports between 2005 and 2018

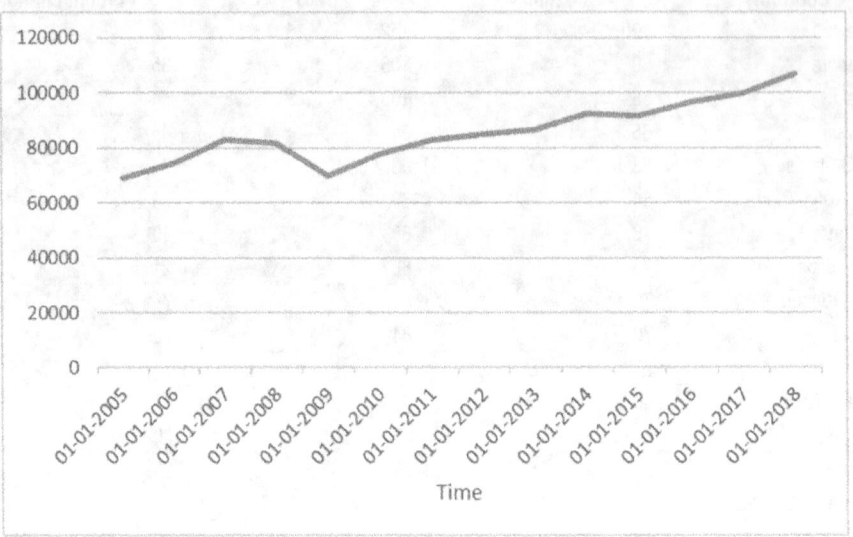

Note: Data source: Eurostat table *mar_mg_am_cvh*- Country level volume (in TEUs) of containers handed in main ports by loading status.
Source: Eurostat.

Industry structure

The container industry has flourished, as ports have been modified to accommodate increasingly large vessels. In 2001, container ships by and large did not carry more than 3,000 containers (Levinson, 2016). During the ensuing decades, container ships became the workhorse for transporting consumer goods (ITF, 2015). In 2010 the largest container ships had a capacity of 13,800 TEUs (Sand, 2020). By 2019, the largest ships had capacities of 23,700 TEUs. Upscaling vessels was attractive to ship-owners in the past, as the cost per box of shipping 10,000 containers was one-half that of shipping 3,000 containers (Levinson, 2020). The economics of container shipping are attractive, as shipping times and costs are advantageous. A container loaded onto a ship in Asia, can arrive in Los Angeles in 23 days; inland rail transportation to Chicago, and then truck transport to Cincinnati, could take an additional 5 days. The cost of the 28-day voyage could be lower than a single business class airline ticket. Whether vessel size will continue to grow remains to be seen, as the cost savings that can be achieved are slowing and significant investment may have to be made by ports to accommodate larger vessels; the point has been reached where societal costs of larger ships are exceeding the private benefits to shipping companies of larger ships (ITF, 2015).

Container freight has also benefited from a number of logistic advantages (Levinson, 2016). The time required to load a large container vessel is a fraction of the time required to load older conventional ships. Reduced storage time and quicker handling has resulted in shorter shipping times from manufacturer to final customer, and enhanced just-in-time manufacturing, which, in turn, has reduced inventory costs. For manufacturers, container shipping was key to supporting growth in global supply chains, thereby resulting in significant increases in trade in intermediate, component products that manufacturers use to make finished goods. Retailers have also benefitted from the higher efficiency of using container shipping, resulting in billions of dollars in cost savings. Moreover, container transport has resulted in spillover cost savings for shippers: packing containers at factories has reduced the need for special packaging to protect cargos from damage or theft; moreover, with containers serving in effect as mobile warehouses, traditional storage costs associated with shipping, have declined. Lower theft had implications for insurance costs, which fell by up to 30%. At the same time, increased vessel size has had an upward effect on shippers' storage costs and insurance costs (ITF, 2015).

While Asia predominates with respect to container trade volumes, the industry itself is more diverse, with APM-Maersk, a company headquartered in Denmark, commanding the top spot with respect to the number of ships being managed, and the share of world capacity. As shown in Table 6, the industry is highly concentrated, with the top 10 firms accounting for 81.2% of capacity in July 2020, and the top 5 accounting for 63.1 %. Consolidation has been occurring in the industry for a number of years. As recently as 2014, the top 10 firms accounted for some 68% of total capacity (ITF, 2018a). Container shipping firms are active in three global alliances that control the large majority of the most important East-West routes, constituting market power with both oligopolistic and oligopsonistic characteristic. In addition, the largest container shipping companies have formed dozens of vessel sharing agreements with each other on many other trade lanes (ITF, 2019b).

Table 2.6. Top 20 container companies, as of 7 July 2020

Company	Country(ies)/economy(ies) of headquarters	Number of ships	Capacity (in TEU) Total (thounsand TEU)	Market share (%)
APM-Maersk	Denmark	685	4 090	17.1
Mediterranean Shg Co	Switzerland, Italy	573	3 820	15.9
COSCO Group	China	494	3 001	12.5
CMA CGM Group	France	534	2 847	11.9
Hapag-Lloyd	Germany	234	1 706	7.1
ONE (Ocean Network Express)	Japan	213	1 552	6.5
Evergreen Line	Chinese Taipei	200	1 291	5.4
HMM Co Ltd	Korea	69	686	2.9
Yang Ming Marine Transport Corp.	Chinese Taipei	92	614	2.6
PIL (Pacific Int. Line)	Singapore	105	332	1.4
Zim	Israel	65	306	1.3
Wan Hai Lines	Chinese Taipei	105	292	1.2
Zhonggu Logistics Corp.	China	115	168	0.7
KMTC	Korea	69	168	0.7
IRISL Group	Iran	47	151	0.6
Antong Holdings (QASC)	China	110	141	0.6
SITC	Hong Kong, China	88	129	0.5
UniFeeder	Denmark	73	110	0.5
X-Press Feeders Group	Singapore	75	106	0.4
TS Lines	Hong Kong, China	44	97	0.4

Source: Alphaliner (2020), Alphaliner Top 100, https://alphaliner.axsmarine.com/PublicTop100/ (accessed on 10 September 2020)

Container companies are seeking to enhance operations by expanding digitization (ITF, 2018b). As noted above, consolidation in the industry is also taking place, as are efforts to expand vertical integration. Many container shipping companies also operate port terminals and logistics operations; the share of carrier-controlled has increased to 35% of all global terminal operations (ITF 2018a). The vertical integration also covers inland logistics, which is a marked departure from previous efforts that relied on outsourcing. Maersk and COSCO, for example, have plans to expand activities to include inland terminals, warehouses and customs brokerage. It has been estimated that up to 80% of Maersk's earnings are tied directly to container shipping, and that the company's plan is to reduce this to 50% in the next few years[5] (UNCTAD, 2019).

Market developments

Volumes of seaborne trade increased annually during 2013 to 2019, with a slight decline expected in 2020 (Table 2.7) (Clarksons Research, 2020). During the period, container trade increased by 27.2% while other modes increased by 15.5%. In 2018 and 2019, the market situation was mixed as weaking trade growth, combined with the delivery of new mega ships, put downward pressure on freight rates in the early months; capacity increased by 6 percent during the year, compared to a 2.6% increase in trade volumes (UNCTAD, 2019). Much of the container trade volume in these two years was carried out on Asia-Europe, Trans-Pacific and Transatlantic routes, with some 60% nevertheless occurring on other, non-mainline routes involving developing countries.

Table 2.7. World seaborne trade, 2013-19, (Millions of tonnes)

Item	2013	2014	2015	2016	2017	2018	2019
Container	1,474	1,557	1,592	1,667	1,763	1,839	1,875
Other modes	8,641	8,932	9,125	9,375	9,734	9,967	9,981
Total	10,115	10,489	10,717	11,042	11,497	11,806	11,856

Source: Clarksons Research, 2020.

The effects of containerization

Containerization greatly reduced the expense of international trade and increased its speed, especially of consumer goods and commodities. It also dramatically changed the character of port cities worldwide. Prior to highly mechanized container transfers, crews of 20–22 dock workers would pack individual cargoes into the hold of a ship. After containerization, large crews of dock workers were no longer necessary at port facilities, and the work force changed drastically.

Containerization does not only refer to the shipping industry, as containers are widely used by trucking and rail transport industries for cargo transport not involving sea transport. Manufacturing also evolved to adapt to take advantage of containers. Companies that once sent small consignments began grouping them into containers. Many cargoes are now designed to fit precisely into containers. The reliability of containers also made just in time manufacturing possible as component suppliers could deliver specific components on regular fixed schedules, although in practice, 50% of the container ships in September 2020 arrived one or more days later than scheduled.

Meanwhile, the port facilities needed to support containerization changed. One effect was the decline of some ports and the rise of others. At the Port of San Francisco, the former piers used for loading and unloading were no longer required, but there was little room to build the vast holding lots needed for container transport. As a result, the Port of San Francisco virtually ceased to function as a major commercial port, but the neighboring port of Oakland emerged as the second largest on the US West Coast. A similar fate met the ports of Manhattan and New Jersey. In the United Kingdom, the Port of London and Port of Liverpool declined in importance. Meanwhile, Britain's Port of Felixstowe and Port of Rotterdam in the Netherlands emerged as major ports. In general, inland ports on waterways incapable of deep-draft ship traffic also declined from containerization in favor of seaports. With intermodal containers, the job of sorting and packing containers could be performed far from the point of embarkation.

Improved cargo security is also an important benefit of containerization. Once the cargo is loaded into a container, it stays there until it reaches its destination. Cargo is securely locked in the container and the doors of the containers are usually sealed. Consequently, cargo is less likely to be stolen or damaged. Recent developments have focused on the use of intelligent logistics optimization to further enhance security (Levinson, 2016).

Risk and Security issues

While the use of containers has enhanced security, limiting opportunities for theft and damage, concerns have been raised over the potential use of containers to facilitate illicit trade. Smugglers have found appealing the ease and low risk of stowing not only counterfeit products, but also drugs and undocumented migrants in the containers. Today smugglers tend to misuse containerized maritime transport in various ways (Box 2.1). Further advantages to smugglers have included the high reliability of container shipping and the anonymity this type of shipping offers.

Box 2.1. Counterfeit trade deception techniques

As mentioned earlier, counterfeiters can use a variety of techniques to avoid detection when shipping products to foreign destinations in container ships. The techniques are adapted to best suit the nature and value of the products involved.

One popular technique involves document falsification. In December 2019, for example, an operation involving the smuggling of counterfeit products from China through the ports of New York and New Jersey was broken up. The operation involved 22 containers of counterfeit sneakers which would have sold for USD 472 million, if they had been genuine. The ship manifests bore false information, describing the merchandise as ventilation fans, vases and plastic hangers. Moreover, the container importers falsely used the identities of legitimate import companies on customs forms, in order to deceive customs brokers and customs officials. While the names of the import companies were legitimate, the phone numbers and email addresses provided were those of the counterfeit importers, who used burner phones and email accounts obtained using false identifiers to conceal their operations. Once cleared by customs, the containers holding counterfeit items were shipped to self-storage facilities, where their contents were broken down, for sale and delivery to wholesalers and retailers. Analysis of customs declarations linked 107 other container shipments to the counterfeit importers, suggesting that a significant volume of counterfeit trade likely passed through the US border undetected.

Another technique involves the physical manipulation of products with a view towards deceiving detection. In 2018, for example, US authorities broke up a New York-based counterfeiting ring which allegedly smuggled nearly 400 000 pairs of counterfeit Air Jordans into the country, potentially costing Nike more than USD 70 million in lost revenue (Rohrlich, 2020). In October 2019, federal agents arrested an individual who purportedly shipped more than USD 5 million worth of fake Timberland and Ugg boots from China into the New York area. In the case of the Air Jordans, the counterfeits were manufactured without any identifying marks; fake logos were added once the shoes cleared customs (Ferrill and Liu, 2020). In the case of the Timberland footwear, counterfeiters attempted to avoid detection by gluing a shoe insert over a fake Timberland logo on the bottom of the boots.

Finally, in some instances, smugglers attempt to avoid detection by concealing illicit goods in a bigger consignment of legitimate items. Not only counterfeiters use this technique. In July 2020, for example, Italian police announced the seizure of 14-tons of the amphetamine drug Captagon made by the Daesh terrorist group in Syria; the USD 1.1 billion seizure was one of the biggest of such drugs in the world (French Press Agency – AFP, 2020). Some 84 million tablets, an amount sufficient to supply the entire European market, were concealed inside industrial goods within containers. Police were required to use chainsaws to cut open the industrial rolling stock and metal gearwheels that the pills were concealed in.

Moreover, customs officials have limited ability to adequately monitor and inspect thousands or more containers that might enter a port on a single ship. With a very large number of containers, and extremely efficient procedures resulting in short turnovers, it becomes in some instances difficult to locate specific containers for further investigation.

In addition, existing enforcement processes rely on a limited number of available techniques and procedures. In fact, available inspection methods that can be applied to screen containers for counterfeits include:

- risk profiling,
- nonintrusive imaging, and
- physical searches.

Importantly, risk profiling and screening are just preliminary checks to determine whether a container needs to be physically inspected or not. The physical search is the only way of effective determining if a container is misused for smuggling of counterfeits.

Risk profiling is based on cargo documents presented in advance to enforcement authorities. Unfortunately, the volume and quality of information presented in these documents is limited, and in many cases can be unreliable. In addition, traffickers are well aware of potential ways of preparing documents in ways that would improve their chances of being highlighted in risk profiling operations, thereby lowering the risk of inspection. This includes for example use of intermediary transit points, in particular free trade zones.

Moreover, the ease of falsifying manifests largely impedes the efficiency of risk profiling of enforcement officials. As noted in the following chapter, key information is still shipped in unsecured way, and there is little progress in adopting modern technologies to address this issue (see Box 3.1. in the following Chapter).

One method for screening imports involved nonintrusive imaging machines, which are used for preselecting of containers for physical searches. These machines use either X-rays or gamma rays to penetrate the container. They provide customs officers with images of the content of a container, which then could lead to a physical inspection. Nonintrusive imaging is very quick and does not require very time-consuming and labor-intensive process of unpacking containers. Unfortunately, the equipment used is expensive, as are operating and maintaining costs (CBO, 2016). Consequently, nonintrusive imaging is not applied widely. Interviews with enforcement official reveal that even in those EU ports where such facilities are the most frequently used, only up to 10% of incoming containers to the EU are scanned. Following these scans, up to 2% of incoming containers are physically searched.

However, as the external features of counterfeit goods barely differ from their legitimate counterparts, scanning of containers is not as effective in detecting counterfeit goods as other types of illegal cargo, such as arms, narcotics or wildlife cargo. Physical searches are the only effective way of concluding if a container contains counterfeits. However, they are also numerous issues related to physical checks.

First, these searches are extremely labor intensive. Inspecting one container can take many hours and require specialized staff, with specialized training. Second, searches require dedicated facilities that are designed for those purposes. The logistics of customs inspection are difficult, as containers are hard to unload, and there is no easy way to inspect a container without unloading it fully.

Physical searches, however, are employed sparingly. Interviews with enforcement officials point that on average less than 2% of containers incoming to the EU are inspected. Importantly, raising of this share seems virtually impossible. A physical inspection of all containers that arrive on a single ship would require tens of thousands of customs inspectors at port (CBO, 2016).

The industry in 2020 (COVID-19)

Industry performance is also being affected by COVID-19, as containment policies have significantly affected the operation of vessels (Heiland and Ulltveit-Moe, 2020). By April 2020, many countries had tightened the rules governing the mobility of sailors arriving in ports. The policies have included restrictions on vessel and crews, such as prohibitions that have curtailed crew changes. With respect to the latter, crew changes are governed by work contracts and labour regulations. Typically, some 100,000 changes take place every month. As of April, some 120 out of 126 economies had implemented restrictions; in 92 countries, changes were prohibited, while in 28 countries such changes were subject to review and approval by authorities. Vessels have in some respects become floating quarantines, as entry into ports is often refused until crews are declared virus-free. The effects are greatest for trips shorter than 14 days, which is the typical quarantine period. In April, about one-third of voyages were 14 days, or longer.

As a result, maritime traffic has slowed. Satellite observation for ships sailing to destinations with restrictions have been down by almost 20% (Heiland and Ulltveit-Moe, 2020). Such disruptions in freight are affecting global supply chains, which have aggravated the challenges facing manufacturers.

Governments have responded by developing specific guidelines for maritime operations. For example, on 27 March 2020, the International Maritime Organization (IMO) provided a series of recommendations to assist governments in managing COVID-19 related issues (IMO, 2020). The 19 recommendations cover four areas:

- *Providing access to berths.* Authorities are encouraged to ensure that vessels have access to berths and that the loading and unloading of cargos is not impeded.
- *Measures to ensure crews changes in ports.* Recommendations include i) designating maritime personnel as essential services and ii) providing such personnel with exemptions from national travel or movement restrictions in order to facilitate crew members from joining or leaving ships.
- *Measures to facilitate port (and related) operations.* Recommendations include i) designating port workers as key workers who provide essential services, ii) ensuring that port personnel have sufficient resources to clear and process cargos, ships and crews and iii) using electronic solutions to minimize risks posed by the interaction or exchange of documents.
- *Measures to ensure health protection in ports.* Recommendations include: i) requesting ships to report COVID-19 infections before arrival in ports; ii) limiting crew departures form ships to those related to crew changes and for medical attention not available on the ship; iii) limiting physical interaction between port and ship personnel and iv) providing seafarer with access to emergency medical services, when needed.

The IMO recommendations have been supplemented by countries, with additional guidelines. In the European Union, *Guidelines on protection of health, repatriation and travel arrangements for seafarers, passengers and other persons on board ships* were issued in a communication published in April 2020 (EC, 2020). In addition to general guidance, the communication covers i) repatriation issues, ii) crew changeovers, iii) designated ports for crew changes, iv) health protection measures and v) ship reporting requirements. Other jurisdictions have, similarly, provided guidance. In the United States, the Center for Disease Control, has provided specific recommendations for preventing the spread of COVID-19 during and after a voyage, including i) personal protective measures, ii) management of sick or exposed persons on board, iii) reporting suspected or confirmed cases and iv) cleaning and disinfection recommendations for common areas on the ship and areas previously occupied by individuals with suspected or confirmed COVID-19 cases (CDC, 2020). In addition, the US Coast Guard has released a series of marine safety information bulletins that provide COVID-19 guidance for the shipping industry.[6]

The Covid-19 crisis has also seen the emergence of "shadow subsidies" in container shipping, that is: transfers from consumers to producers that result from constraints on competition contained in shipping regulation. Confronted with reduction in demand for containerized trade, the main container carriers withdrew ship capacity by cancelling scheduled voyages, so called "blank sailings". Between February and June 2020, approximately 20 to 30% of the container ship capacity on the main trade lanes was idled [7]. The artificially created scarcity pushed up the price to ship a container. Freight rates rose particularly strongly on the Trans-Pacific trade lane, but many other trade routes also saw significant increases despite the drop in containerised trade volumes (Figure 2.2).

As a result of these remarkable shifts in the freight rates, container carriers made large profits in the first half of 2020. The profit margin of ten main container carriers over the second quarter of 2020 was 8.5%, the highest since the third quarter of 2010, according to Alphaliner. [8]

Figure 2.2. Containerised ocean freight rates developments per week in selected trade lanes

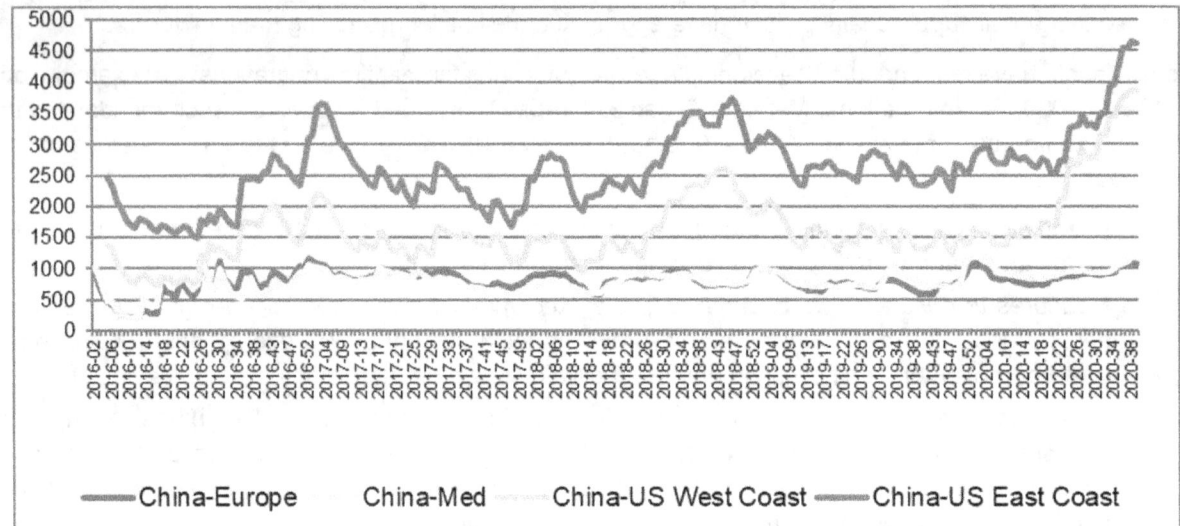

Note: Shanghai Containerised Freight Index: spot rate (USD) to ship a container from Shanghai to North Europe, Med, US West Coast and US East Coast. Source: International Transport Forum based on data from Shanghai Shipping Exchange

These profits could be viewed as a shadow subsidy paid for by consumers. This shadow subsidy comes on top of state support in some cases: at least four of the main container carriers have also benefited from the Covid-19 aid for the shipping sector. This development raises concern for competition authorities. Chinese authorities have recently asked carriers for explanations and requested that they re-instate cancelled services on the Trans-Pacific trade lane. [9] In the United States, the Federal Maritime Commission has also announced to investigate the blank sailing strategy of carriers. [10] At the time of writing, the European Commission had not (yet) taken action. [11] (ITF, 2020b).

References

Alphaliner (2020), Alphaliner Top 100, https://alphaliner.axsmarine.com/PublicTop100/ (accessed 9 July 2020).

CDC (2020), Interim Guidance for Ships on Managing Suspected or Confirmed Cases of Coronavirus Disease 2019 (COVID-19) United States Center for Disease Control and Prevention, https://www.cdc.gov/quarantine/maritime/recommendations-for-ships.html.

Clarksons Research (2020), Seaborne Trade Monitor: Volume 7, No. 7, Clarkson Research Services Limited, London.

EC (2020), Communication from the Commission: Guidelines on protection of health, repatriation and travel arrangements for seafarers, passengers and other persons on board ships, C(2020) 3100 final, European Commission, Brussels, https://ec.europa.eu/transport/sites/transport/files/legislation/c20203100.pdf.

Ferrill, E. and E. Liu (2020), New Legislation Would Empower U.S. Customs to Seize Products Infringing Design Patents at the U.S. Border, Finnegan, Henderson, Farabow, Garrett & Dunner, LLP, https://www.finnegan.com/en/insights/articles/new-legislation-would-empower-us-customs-to-seize-products-infringing-design-patents-at-the-us-border.html

French Press Agency – AFP (2020), "Italy seizes Daesh-made drugs worth $1.1 billion", Daily Sabah, https://www.dailysabah.com/world/europe/italy-seizes-daesh-made-drugs-worth-11-billion.

Heiland, I. and K. Ulltveit-Moe (2020), An unintended crisis: COVID-19 restrictions hit sea transportation, VoxEU, https://voxeu.org/article/covid-19-restrictions-hit-sea-transportation.

IMO (2020), Coronavirus (COVID-19) – Preliminary list of recommendations for Governments and relevant national authorities on the facilitation of maritime trade during the COVID-19 pandemic, Circular Letter No.4204/Add.6, 27 March 2020, International Maritime Organization, London, www.imo.org/en/MediaCentre/HotTopics/Documents/Circular%20Letter%20No.4204Add.6%20%20Coronavirus%20Covid-19%20Preliminary%20List%20Of%20Recommendations.pdf .

ITF (2015), "The Impact of Mega-Ships", International Transport Forum Policy Papers, No. 10, OECD Publishing, Paris, https://doi.org/10.1787/5jlwvzcm3j9v-en.

ITF (2020), "Transport infrastructure investment and maintenance", ITF Transport Statistics (database), https://doi.org/10.1787/g2g55573-en (accessed on February 2020).

ITF (2018a), "The Impact of Alliances in Container Shipping", International Transport Forum, OECD, https://www.itf-oecd.org/sites/default/files/docs/impact-alliances-container-shipping.pdf

ITF (2018b), "Information Sharing for more Efficient Maritime Logistics", International Transport Forum, OECD, https://www.itf-oecd.org/sites/default/files/docs/information-sharing-maritime-logistics.pdf

ITF (2019b), "Container Shipping in Europe; Data for the Evaluation of the EU Consortia Block Exemption', International Transport Forum, OECD, https://www.itf-oecd.org/sites/default/files/docs/container-shipping-europe-eu-consortia_3.pdf

ITF (2020b), "Lessons from COVID-19 State Support for Maritime Shipping", COVID-19 Transport Brief, International Transport Forum, OECD, https://www.itf-oecd.org/sites/default/files/shipping-state-support-covid-19.pdf

Journal of Commerce Staff (2019), "Top 50 global port rankings 2018", Journal of Commerce, 9 August 2020, https://www.joc.com/port-news/top-50-global-port-rankings-2018_20190809.html.

Levinson, M. (2016), The Box: How the Shipping Container Made the World Smaller and the World Economy Bigger, Princeton University Press, Princeton, NJ

Rohrlich, J. (2020), How $470 million worth of fake Nikes get into the US, Quartz Media Inc., https://qz.com/1778276/how-counterfeit-nikes-get-into-the-us/.

Rushton, A., Croucher, P. and Baker, P. (2017), The Handbook of Logistics and Distribution Management, Sixth edition, Kogan Page Ltd, London.

Sand, P., (2020), The 2010s: A Decade of Market Imbalance and Ultra Large Container Ships, BIMCO, Copenhagen, https://www.bimco.org/news/market_analysis/2020/20200702_the_2010_decade_of_market_imbalance.

Scerra, M. (2020), Container Shipping - Statistics & Facts, Statista GmbH, Hamburg, https://www.statista.com/topics/1367/container-shipping/.

UNCTAD (2020), "Liner shipping connectivity index, annual", UNCTADSTAT (dataset), United Nations Conference on Trade and Development, https://unctadstat.unctad.org/wds/TableViewer/tableView.aspx?ReportId=92, accessed August, 2020.

UNCTAD (2019), Review of Maritime Transport 2019, United Nations Publications, New York, https://unctad.org/en/PublicationsLibrary/rmt2019_en.pdf.

World Bank (2020), "Container port traffic (TEU: 20 foot equivalent units)", DataBank (dataset), The World Bank Group, https://data.worldbank.org/indicator/IS.SHP.GOOD.TU, accessed 13 August 2020.

WTO (2019), World Trade Statistical Review 2019, World Trade Organization, Geneva, http://www.wto.org/english/res_e/statis_e/wts2019_e/wts2019_e.pdf.

3 Containerships: legal frameworks and threats of illicit trade

International maritime transport in container ships has been framed with a number of international rules and norms. In addition, the misuse of maritime transport in illicit trade is a concern of both governments and industry. They have been active in combating counterfeiting and piracy on a number of fronts, both independently and, equally importantly, with each other. Besides efforts undertaken in a national context, governments have been working through multilateral institutions and on a bilateral and regional basis to address these issues. Industry has also been active, nationally and internationally, both on a sectoral and cross-sectoral basis.

This chapter provides information on the legal frameworks governing seaborne trade, including presentation of the Hague-Visby Rules, Bill of Lading, Rotterdam Rules and legal standards that frame the containerized transport. This chapter also outlines the existing legal frameworks that directly or indirectly counter specific threats posed by illicit trade in maritime transport.

Hague-Visby Rules

The so-called Hague–Visby Rules is a set of international rules that frame carriage of cargo transport by sea. Initially they were known as the Hague rules, with the official title: "International Convention for the Unification of Certain Rules of Law relating to Bills of Lading". After the 1968 amendment (the "Protocol to Amend the International Convention for the Unification of Certain Rules of Law Relating to Bills of Lading", known as Brussel amendment) the Hague Rules became colloquially referred to as the Hague–Visby Rules.

The rules apply to carriers and shippers and cargo owners, and set the minimum duties of carriers and shippers and cargo owners.

The rules set a list of main duties of carries, including to "*properly and carefully load, handle, stow, carry, keep, care for, and discharge the goods carried*" to "*exercise due diligence to ... make the ship seaworthy*" and to "*... properly man, equip and supply the ship*". According to the Rules, shippers are obliged to pay freight, to pack the goods sufficiently for the journey, and to have the goods ready for shipment as agreed. Importantly the shipper must also describe the goods honestly and accurately, and not to ship dangerous cargo (unless agreed by both parties).

Importantly, Hague-Visby Rules do not set strict duties, instead set requirements for reasonable standards of professionalism. In addition, the rules include a wide range of situations exempting parties from liability on a cargo claim.

Bill of Lading (BOL)

The Bill of Lading is the evidence of receipt, introduced by the Hague-Visby Rules. It is a document issued by a carrier that acknowledges receipt of cargo for shipment by sea. It is a critical document used in international trade to ensure that exporters receive payments and importers receive the goods.

The primary use of the bill of lading is a receipt issued by the carrier once the goods have been loaded onto the vessel. This receipt can be used as proof of shipment for customs and insurance purposes. Hence, the BOL and the information it contains become the key input into risk profiling carried out by the enforcement officials. Consequently, it is essential that the information on BOLs be up to date and accurate.

Currently, there are cases where there is no correspondence between the description filed by shipper and the actual goods shipped. In cases of full compliance, a "clean bill of lading" is used. A "dirty bill of lading" is issued if the goods to be shipped differ in quality or quantity from the contract description, and a "STC" ("container Said To Contain") is issued if the cargo cannot be effectively examined (e.g. the container is sealed). In that case the carrier issues a BOL referring to goods as "container (identified by number) said to contain".

A possible way to address the problem of inadequacies of information in BOL, would be an electronic bill of lading, with transparent ways of data handling. Proposals to utilize this have existed for quite some time, the adoption progress has been very slow (Box 3.1)

Box 3.1. Electronic BOL

An electronic bill of lading could be a potential solution to challenges surrounding data accuracy in the BOL description. It would also offer reductions in costs and the time required to prepare paper bills of lading. An electronic BOL is the legal and functional equivalent of a paper BOL that replicates its core functions – it acts as receipt and can be presented as evidence to enforcement officials.

The processes for introducing BOLs globally tend to be very slow. Some economies lack legislation that would enable introduction of electronic BOLs, others still need specific legal solutions to such regulations. In addition, there are issues with co-ordination of efforts. Generally, the lack of commonly agreed safe standard seems to be an obstacle.

In this context, new technologies such as Blockchain might be leveraged to speed up progress of adopting electronic BOLs. Such modern technological solutions could be also used in an e-BOL environment to prevent forgery, as well as facilitate keeping e-BOLs up to date, in light of the growing number of actors, and the fast pace of modern container trade.

Rotterdam Rules

To meet the rapidly evolving phenomenon of containerization, a new treaty including a new set of rules was adopted by the United Nations.

The "United Nations Convention on Contracts for the International Carriage of Goods Wholly or Partly by Sea" (knows as "Rotterdam Rules") proposes new international rules to revise the legal framework for maritime affreightment and carriage of goods by sea. The Rules primarily address the legal relationship between carriers and cargo-owners. They establish a comprehensive, binding, uniform legal regime governing the rights and obligations of shippers, carriers and consignees under a contract for door-to-door shipments that involve international sea transport.

The convention was adopted by the UN General Assembly on 11 December 2008. The process of ratification by countries has been rather slow, as of September 2020 the rules have been ratified by only five countries: Benin, Cameroun, Congo, Spain and Togo.

Multimodal containers – legal settings

There are several international conventions that frame international maritime container trade, including:

- Customs Convention on Containers (CCC)
- Convention for Safe Containers (CSC)
- Istanbul Convention
- BIC-CODE

The Customs Convention on Containers (CCC), signed in 1972 is administered by the World Customs Organization. It provides for the temporary importation of containers, free of import duties and taxes, subject to re-exportation within 3 months and without the production of customs or security documents. The Convention also provides for the approval of containers under customs seal.

The Convention for Safe Containers (CSC) provides uniform international safety regulations, equally applicable to all modes of surface transport. It decrees that every container travelling internationally be fitted with a CSC Safety-approval Plate. This holds essential information about the container, including age, registration number, dimensions and weights, as well as its strength and maximum stacking capability.

The Istanbul Convention, adopted in 1990 and administered by the WCO regulates the temporary admission of goods into a Customs territory with relief from duties and taxes.

From the private sector, the Bureau International des Containers et du Transport Intermodal (BIC) oversees standards for intermodal containers, commonly referred to as "shipping containers". It aims at promotion of cooperation among corporations, governments and independent organizations relating to intermodal freight transport, the process of containerization, and the transport and handling of shipping containers. BIC was established in 1933 under the auspices of the International Chamber of Commerce

In 1970, the BIC developed the international system for containers marking known as the 'BIC-CODE' system, adopted by the International Organization for Standardization (ISO) in 1972.

Since the mid-1980s, the BIC has also been involved in the development of combined transport (rail-road and barge-road). With its considerable experience in promoting the expansion of containerization, the BIC has been involved at regional and international levels in the further development of this form of intermodal transport.

The BIC has also contributed to the development and updating of the above-mentioned international conventions, which have contributed to the tremendous expansion of containerization.

Legal frameworks to counter illicit trade in maritime transport

In the specific context of misuse of containerized maritime transport, several initiatives have been taken by the public and private sectors to monitor and to limit misuse. These initiatives include:

- Improvement of information sharing,
- Standard setting, and
- Industry declarations of intent.

Information sharing

UNODC/WCO

The United Nations Office on Drugs and Crime (UNDOC) and the World Customs Organization (WCO) launched a UNODC-WCO Container Control Programme (CCP) in 2004 (UNODC, 2020). The main purpose of the programme is to facilitate the tracking of containers from the port of origin to the port of destination, by collecting the information on the routes of the freight containers through CSM data.

ConTraffic

ConTraffic is a project developed by the European Commission – Joint Research Center in collaboration with the European Antifraud Office (OLAF) and the Directorate General for Taxation and Customs Union (DG TAXUD) (JRC, 2020). It aims at supporting customs authorities dealing with the control of containerised cargo, by developing novel methods and information technology (IT) tools that assist authorities in their risk assessment activities, based on Container Status Messages (CSM) that describes the status and movement of the containers.

The front end of ConTraffic is a web site, which provides access to a number of online services:

- "Track and Trace" allows users to get CSM information on one or more containers in a specified time period or in real time.
- Container Surveillance tracks in near real-time the movements of specific containers entered in the system by the users. The application notifies (by email) the users of any detected new movements of the containers they have been entered for tracking.
- Port2Port shows the results of pre-computed statistical analysis on the logistic routes followed by carriers to transport containers between particular departure and destination ports. The graphs for the pre-calculated pair or departure-destination ports (of a particular carrier) show which routes have been used by the carrier over a period of time and with what frequency, identifying any possible outliers (i.e. abnormal routes).
- Visual Analytics is an application that allows users to interactively explore all the data in the ConTraffic database. A Visual Analytics session entails selection of the data to be displayed, followed by the visualisation of the selected data; the data are then further refined, leading to new visualisations. Once the selection criteria have been set, the selected information is visualized as a geographical map, timelines and text tables. The map shows the spatial distribution of the selected information. Symbols are represented at some locations where information has been found. For each container, several timelines are shown, depending on the selected information.

The container-shipping sector has been active in digitalisation, leading to industry-driven platforms such as Tradelens and standard setting via the Digital Container Shipping Association. Although these initiatives could raise competition concerns especially when they lock in customers (ITF, 2018b), they could also possibly help shipping companies to use their pivotal role to better scrutinise their cargo. These digital projects could help to improve the traceability of cargo and its characteristics, including its legality. That way, shipping companies could show they are serious about implementing due diligence on the cargo they transport (Merk, 2020).

Seaports should also up their game and improve their capability for effective scrutiny of cargo. Several ports have created Wildlife Traffic Monitoring Units to detect and prevent the illegal transport of wildlife. Seaports should also include combating illegal timber and wildlife trade as objectives in their sustainability strategies and be accountable for their actions on this (Merk, 2020).

Standard setting

The International Standards Organization

The International Standards Organization (ISO) is an independent, non-governmental international organization with a membership of 164 national standards bodies (ISO 2020a). Through its members, it brings together experts to share knowledge and develop voluntary, consensus-based, market relevant international standards that support innovation and provide solutions to global challenges (ISO, 2020a).

A number of standards contribute to the effective running of the shipping industry, through its dedicated committee on ships and marine technology (ISO, 2017). The committee works closely with the International Maritime Organization (IMO) to ensure that its standards respect and contribute to meeting IMO regulations (ISO, 2017).

ISO standards are also instrumental in helping to connect ports with rail hubs, air freights and land-based distribution networks, offering greater efficiency in how goods are moved. Because ISO standards are a powerful tool to ensure collaboration and efficiency across the supply chain, they make an important contribution to connecting ships, ports and people (ISO, 2017).

Standardization Activity: ISO/TC 204 Intelligent Transport Systems

This standardization concerns information, communication and control systems, including intermodal and multimodal aspects thereof, traveller information, traffic management, public transport, commercial transport, emergency services and commercial services in the intelligent transport systems (ITS) field (ISO, 1992; ISO, 2019). ISO/TC 204 is responsible for the overall system aspects and infrastructure aspects of intelligent transport systems, as well as the co-ordination of the overall ISO work programme in this field, including the schedule for standards development (ISO, 1992; ISO, 2019).

Transport telematics at the worldwide level are being addressed mainly by technical committee ISO/TC 204 Intelligent Transport Systems (ISO, 1992; ISO, 2019). Standards concerning global trade involving container ships and maritime transport cover the security of intermodal freight, the transport of dangerous goods, real time tracking of transported goods and on-board computing and mobile communication with vehicles (Baldini et al., 2015).

Working Groups (WG) for container transportation include in particular (Baldini et al., 2015):

- WG1 - Architecture
- WG3 - TICS database technology
- WG4 - Automatic vehicle and equipment identification
- WG7 - General fleet management and commercial/freight
- WG9 - Integrated transport information, management and control systems
- WG11 - Route guidance and navigation systems

Standardization Activity: ISO TC 8 Maritime.

This committee deals with the design, construction, training, structural elements, outfitting parts, equipment, methods and technology, and marine environmental matters that are used in shipbuilding. It covers sea-going ships, vessels for inland navigation, offshore structures, ship-to-shore interface, the operation of ships, marine structures subject to IMO requirements and the observation and exploration of the sea (ISO, 2020b). Of particular relevance is:

Standard: ISO 17363:2013 Supply chain applications of RFID – Freight containers

This standard prescribes the usage of read/write radio-frequency identification (RFID) cargo shipment-specific tags associated with containerized freight for supply chain management purposes (Baldini et al., 2015). It defines the air interface communications, a common set of required data structures, and a commonly organized, through common syntax and semantics, set of optional data requirements (ISO, 2013); it:

- makes recommendations about a second-generation supply chain tag intended to monitor the condition and security of a freight resident within a freight container;
- specifies the implementation of sensors for a freight resident in a freight container;
- makes specific recommendations about mandatory non-reprogrammable information on the shipment tag;
- makes specific recommendations about the data link interface for GPS or GLS services;
- specifies the reuse and recyclability of the RF tag;
- specifies the means by which the data in a compliant RF tag is "backed-up" by bar codes and two-dimensional symbols, as well as human-readable information.

In addition, there are a number of pilot projects being conducted on secure shipping containers that not only can be tracked but contain sensors that show whether a container has been tampered with at any point in the supply chain.

ASTM International

ASTM International, formerly known as American Society for Testing and Materials, is a globally recognized leader in the development and delivery of voluntary consensus standards for a wide range of materials, products, systems, and services. (ASTM, 2020a). Membership in the organization is open to anyone with an interest in its activities, and is upon request, not by appointment nor by invitation. Standards are developed within committees, and new committees are formed as needed, upon request of interested members. ASTM International has no mandate nor role in requiring or enforcing compliance with its standards.

Today, there are more than 140 countries participating in ASTM International. There are over 12,000 ASTM standards used around the world to improve product quality, enhance health and safety, strengthen market access and trade, and build consumer confidence (ASTM, 2020a).

With respect to counterfeit trade involving maritime trade, the following ASTM standards are relevant:

Standard: ASTM D5728-12: New Guide for Examination of Counterfeit Documents.

This guide provides procedures that should be used by forensic document examiners to determine whether a document is genuine or counterfeit (ASTM, 2020b). These procedures are applicable to the visual and mechanical examinations and comparisons of questioned documents to known authentic standards (ASTM, 2020b).

This standard does not purport to address all safety concerns, if any, associated with its use. It is the responsibility of the user of this standard to establish appropriate safety and health practices and determine the applicability of regulatory limitations prior to use (ASTM, 2020b).

Standard: ASTM D5728-12 Standard Practices for Securement of Cargo in Intermodal and Unimodal Surface Transport

This standard refers to sources that provide detailed information on the loading, blocking, bracing, and unloading of specific types of cargo in unimodal and intermodal transport. Some of these sources are proprietary, while others are massive and complex in scope; none are consistently provided to shippers, carriers, and consignees (ASTM, 2012). Many of the losses experienced by cargo in transport are due to the failure to practice proper basic cargo handling and loading techniques.

This standard is intended to outline those techniques in simple, clear, generic, and easy to promulgate formats, including posters, slides, videotapes, and pamphlets, and are further intended to serve as the basis upon which a comprehensive cargo handling methodology may be built (ASTM, 2012). Users of these practices should avail themselves of the detailed resource information available.

Even though standard ASTM D5728-12 does not seem directly related to trade in counterfeit goods, it refers to types of information that could be used to screen for potential infiltration by traffickers, including presence of counterfeits.

Industry declarations of intent

There are several industry initiatives dedicated to reinforcing supply chains and raising awareness to counter illicit trade. Two are of particular relevance in the context of misuse of containerized maritime transport:

- United for Wildlife Transport Taskforce's Buckingham Palace Declaration, and
- Declaration of Intent to Prevent the Maritime Transportation of Counterfeit Goods

United for Wildlife Transport Taskforce's Buckingham Palace Declaration

The United for Wildlife Transport Taskforce's Buckingham Palace Declaration (BPD) has been signed by a wide range of stakeholders committed to combatting wildlife crime, and counter the misuse of maritime transport in wildlife trafficking. Signatories of BPD include transport organizations and associations (incl. IATA, International Chamber of Shipping, IMO), governmental agencies (including UK Foreign and Commonwealth Office, Dubai customs), non-governmental organizations (e.g. Traffic and WWF), and individuals companies, including maritime operator. This initiative has produced positive results, including the creation of information-sharing systems, and publication of best practices for transport operators.

Closer to the scope of this report, the BDP has inspired the development of the Declaration of Intent to Prevent the Maritime Transportation of Counterfeit Goods.

Declaration of Intent to Prevent the Maritime Transportation of Counterfeit Goods

In 2016 leaders from global shipping firms, freight forwarders and brand owners whose products are counterfeited agreed on a joint "Declaration of Intent to Prevent the Maritime Transport of Counterfeit Goods" (ICC BASCAP, 2016).

The declaration marked the first time the global shipping industry and brand owners had made a public commitment to work together to stop the transport of counterfeit goods on shipping vessels (The Maritime Executive, 2016). Signatories include two leading global shipping firms, two freight forwarders and ten major multinational brand manufacturers, along with the International Federation of Freight Forwarders Associations (FIATA) and two ICC groups (the Business Action to Stop Counterfeiting and Piracy and the Commercial Crime Service). The signatories of the declaration in the maritime and transport industries include shipping companies: Maersk Line, CMA CGM Group, MSN and Arkas, as well as freight forwarding and logistics companies -- Kuehne and Nagel and Expeditors.

The declaration acknowledges the "destructive impact" of counterfeits on international trade, and encourages signatories to embrace a zero tolerance for counterfeiting and to collaborate through joint working groups in order to develop a detailed series of non-binding measures or best practices in five areas aimed at:

- Implementation of all applicable international, regional and national rules and mutually agreed standards aimed at preventing the carriage of counterfeit products;
- Reinforcement of supply chain controls, including the application of appropriate due diligence measures, such as "Know Your Customer processes";
- Improving risk profiling;
- Raising awareness and conducting training; and
- Enhancing information sharing and co-operation.

The declaration is nonbinding, relying on the signatories to make their best efforts to achieve the goals of the agreement:

> "This Declaration of Intent is a voluntary and non-binding statement of the signatories' mutual intent to prevent, to the best of their abilities, to the extent possible and in compliance with all applicable laws including competition laws, the maritime transportation of counterfeit goods. The Declaration of Intent is not intended to create any legally enforceable rights or obligations in respect of any signatory, including any obligation on their part to enter into any additional binding agreements."

Information sharing and risk profiling

One of the more effective ways to manage containerised cargo is through information-based risk analysis (Baldini et al., 2015). This can help customs authorities worldwide to target high-risk shipments and proceed with physical checks.

The standard procedures for risk analysis and controls performed by customs are based on the following components (Baldini et al., 2015):

- information about the entities involved (shipper, consignee, customs broker, agent, etc.);
- characteristics of the goods (tariff classification, value, weight, etc.); and
- other information provided by the entities involved, including the origin, destination, and routes of cargos, including transhipment points.

However, in most cases, authorities have very limited or incomplete information about the actual global routes of containerized cargos and they do not have data that describe the itinerary, status and movement of shipping containers in a systematic way. Shippers, however, collect and store Container Status Messages (CSM). These records describe the global movement and status of containers and provide an independent source of information, which complements the information available to customs and other authorities. CSM data could thus be used to help reconstruct the route of containers, contributing importantly to route-based risk analysis, in support of investigations.

Points C. and E. of the declaration address this as follows:

> *Point C: Risk profiling*
>
> *Apply specific vigilance measures and common early warning indicators in order to identify high-risk shipments of counterfeits.*
>
> *Co-operate in order to review and refine, when appropriate, pre-agreed criteria by all signatories for screening and early warning indicators of counterfeits.*
>
> *Point E: Sharing information and co-operating*

> *Identify a point of contact for each signatory to co-ordinate with national and supra-national authorities.*
>
> *Support processes developed by competent authorities such as the World Customs Organization and national customs agencies to aid in the detection and seizure of counterfeit products.*
>
> *Contribute to information exchanges between the parties on detection and seizure of counterfeit products, subject to compliance with i) signatory's relevant contractual obligations, such as those pertaining to confidentiality of customer information, and ii) applicable laws and regulations, including, but not limited to, competition and data protection laws.*
>
> *Co-operate and collaborate with competent law enforcement authorities on investigations relating to the carriage of counterfeits.*

Reinforcing supply chain controls and raising awareness

While risk profiling can be highly useful to combat counterfeiting, by helping public authorities to identify abnormal trade routes, it does not provide any information on the exact content of these shipments, and are only helpful when the cargo shipped by containers is known to the authorities.

Another way to fight against counterfeit seaborne trade is to reinforce supply chain controls. The declaration highlights the different areas that need to be addressed in Section C:

> *Point C: Supply chain controls*
>
> *Apply appropriate due diligence measures, such as "Know Your Customer processes".*
>
> *Include appropriate conditions prohibiting the carriage of counterfeit products.*
>
> *Take appropriate steps in order to ensure there is no co-operation with companies, entities or individuals with serious or proven involvement in counterfeiting.*
>
> *Encourage, wherever deemed appropriate by the signatory, the implementation of similar measures by other players in the extended supply chains.*

Application of all applicable international, regional and national rules and mutually agreed standards: a zero-tolerance policy regarding counterfeiting

There are numerous international, regional and national rules and mutually agreed standards aimed at combatting the carriage of counterfeit products. One of the key provisions of the 2016 ICC/BASCAP declaration is to encourage industry to apply these instruments, to the maximum extent possible. Point A of the declaration provides guidance on how this can be achieved:

> *Point A. A zero-tolerance policy regarding counterfeiting*
>
> *Implement applicable international, regional and national rules and mutually agreed standards aimed at preventing the carriage of counterfeit products.*
>
> *Inform all customers and sub-contractors of these commitments and our zero-tolerance policy towards counterfeits.*
>
> *Ensure compliance with all applicable laws, regulations and rules including, but not limited to, those relating to customs regulation"*

Shipping lines and the majority of brand owners who signed the declaration in 2016 remain committed to collaborate with respect to risk profiling and control of the supply chain.

References

ASTM (2012), ASTM D5728-12: Standard Practices for Securement of Cargo in Intermodal and Unimodal Surface Transport, ASTM International, West Conshohocken, PA, 2012, www.astm.org

ASTM (2020a), About US, American Society for Testing and Materials, ASTM International, West Conshohocken, PA, 2012 https://www.astm.org/ABOUT/overview.html

ASTM (2020b), ASTM WK19398: New Guide for Examination of Counterfeit Documents, ASTM International, West Conshohocken, PA, https://www.astm.org/DATABASE.CART/WORKITEMS/WK19398.htm

Baldini G., I. Nai Fovino, R. Satta, A. Tsois, E. Checchi, 2015; Survey of techniques for the fight against counterfeit goods and Intellectual Property Rights (IPR) infringement; EUR 27688 EN; doi:10.2788/97231

ICC BASCAP (2016), Declaration of Intent to prevent the maritime transportation of counterfeit goods, https://iccwbo.org/content/uploads/sites/3/2017/04/ICC-Declaration-of-Intent-to-prevent-the-maritime-transportation-of-counterfeit-goods.pdf

ISO (2019), ITS Standardization Activities of ISO/TC 204, International Organization for Standardization, Geneva, Switzerland.

ISO (2013), ISO 17363: Supply chain applications of RFID — Freight containers, International Organization for Standardization, Geneva, Switzerland. https://www.iso.org/standard/57596.html

ISO (2017), Moving Goods With Iso Standards, International Organization for Standardization, Geneva, Switzerland, https://www.iso.org/news/ref2227.html

ISO (2020b), ISO/TC 8: Ships and marine technology International Organization for Standardization, Geneva, Switzerland, https://www.iso.org/committee/45776.html

ITF (2019b), "Container Shipping in Europe; Data for the Evaluation of the EU Consortia Block Exemption', International Transport Forum, OECD, https://www.itf-oecd.org/sites/default/files/docs/container-shipping-europe-eu-consortia_3.pdf

JRC (2020), ConTraffic online services, European Comission – Joint research Center https://contraffic.jrc.ec.europa.eu/

Merk, O. (2020), "How shipping can help to avoid pandemics", Transport Policy Matters, International Transport Forum, OECD, https://transportpolicymatters.org/2020/10/08/how-shipping-can-help-to-avoid-pandemics/

The Maritime Executive (2016), Shipping Takes on Counterfeit Goods Trade, https://www.maritime-executive.com/article/shipping-takes-on-counterfeit-goods-trade

UNODC, 2020, https://www.unodc.org/unodc/en/ccp/ccp-programme-details.html

4 Containerships and global trade in fake products – the Evidence

This chapter presents quantitative evidence on the misuse of containerships in the trade of counterfeit and pirated goods across global markets. While the challenges of intercepting counterfeit products transported in containers are significant, shipments of counterfeits are nevertheless intercepted by authorities.

As indicated earlier, counterfeiters are using a number of techniques to escape prosecution i) by covering infringing trademarks and then removing the covering after the counterfeit goods have cleared customs, ii) by shipping infringing trademarks separately from goods and iii) by hiding counterfeit items in ways that make them virtually impossible to detect. With respect to legislation to facilitate enforcement in such instances was introduced in the United States in December 2019. If enacted, customs authorities would be given discretionary power to enforce recorded US design patents; this would enable seizure of covered items, even if there were no trademark infringement.

Where do we source our information?

Customs seizures of IP-infringing goods

All information concerning trade in counterfeit and pirated trade comes from the OECD database on customs seizures (OECD/EUIPO, 2019) (see Box 4.1 for more details).

The descriptive analysis of the dataset of customs seizures presented in the OECD-EUIPO study identified 184 provenance economies[12] of counterfeit and pirated products between 2014 and 2016, as compared to 173 for the 2011-13 period (OECD/EUIPO, 2019). The study also noted that some modes of transport tend to dominate the others in terms of the total number of seizures. In addition, some provenance economies may specialise in certain modes of transport, types of goods.

The analysis carried out in the present study highlights some important measurement and data-related issues. [13] Even though the information on counterfeit and pirated trade has improved significantly in recent years, more can be done to improve and expand information on this phenomenon. In the EU, for example, data collection focuses on seizures done at the external borders. Consequently, the information on the production of fakes within the EU for the internal market and on the circulations of fakes within the EU is less precise.

> **Box 4.1. The OECD database on seized counterfeit and pirated products**
>
> The database on customs seizures is the critical quantitative input to this study. This database brings together data from three separate datasets: the European Commission's Directorate-General for Taxation and Customs Union (DG TAXUD) the US Customs and Border Protection (CBP) and the World Customs Organization (WCO). The database includes detailed information on seizures of IP-infringing goods made by customs officers in 99 economies around the world between 2011 and 2016. For each year, there are more than 100 000 observations in the database; in most cases, each individual observation corresponds to one customs seizure.
>
> The database contains a wealth of information about IP-infringing goods that can be used for quantitative and qualitative analysis. In most cases, for each seizure the database details: the date of seizure, the mode of transport of the fake products, the departure and destination economies, the general statistical category of the goods seized and a detailed description of the goods, the name of legitimate brand owner, the number of products seized and their approximate value. [14]
>
> For more information on the OECD database see OECD/EUIPO (2019).

Importantly, the main goal of this exercise is to understand the nature of misuse of containerships in the global trade in counterfeit and pirated goods. Given the dynamic character of trade flows in containerships, more research and more data are needed to fully understand some additional dimensions.

Data on containerships trade

The data for trade via container ships is based on specialized datasets on maritime trade volumes and values. Several databases are used in this analysis, including:

- OECD International Transport Forum (ITF) database,
- Eurostat Comext,
- Indices on containerized maritime transport developed by UNCTAD (United Nations Conference of Trade and Development).

The first source of data is the OECD International Transport Forum (ITF, 2020), which collects on an annual basis data on investment and maintenance spending on transport infrastructure from all its member countries. Data are collected from Transport Ministries, statistical offices and other institutions designated as official data sources. This database includes two variables that are useful for the economic analysis: the value of maritime port infrastructure investment and the weight of exports through maritime containers transport by year for numerous economies worldwide.

The second source of data is the Eurostat's reference database for detailed statistics on international trade in goods: Comext (Comext, 2020). It provides access not only to data of the EU and its individual Member States but also to statistics of a significant number of non-EU countries. This includes notably information on the volume and value of trade in genuine goods by economies, mode of transports and type of goods.

Last, the analysis employs three indices on containerized maritime transport developed by UNCTAD (United Nations Conference of Trade and Development), including Liner shipping connectivity indices (LSCI), and container-port trafic index.

The LSCI indices are composit measures based on six components, each one capturing a dimension of a country's or port's "connectivity". These dimentions include:

- The number of carriers that provide services from and to a specific port or ports in a specific economy. The more companies are active in given economy (or port), the more choice of transport is offered and the more connected this economy (or port) becomes.
- The size of the largest ship that is deployed to provide services in the analysed port or analysed economy. This captures maximum capacity of the port, and hence proxies its infrastructure, accessibility and equipment.
- The number of direct services that connect to other economies.
- The total number of ships that are deployed on services to serve analysed port(s).
- The total container carrying capacity of the analysed port(s).
- The number of other economies that are connected to the country through direct liner shipping services.

The LSCI indices are calclulated for both individual ports and economies. LSCI indices are based on private data, sent by liner shipping companies. These aggregated indicators are constructed for individual ports, and whole economies. In this study, two LSCI indices are used:

- Port LSCI, which presents connectivity of individual ports in an economy.
- Bilateral LSCI, which indicates a country pair's integration level into global liner shipping networks.

In addition, the analysis also uses UNCTAD's container port traffic index. This index measures the flow of containers from land to sea transport modes and vice versa. This index is constructed for individual ports, relative to the port with the most intense traffic.

Regarding both types of indices – LSCI and the container port traffic index – the general rule of thumb is that economies with high values are actively involved in containerized trade. Consequently, China usually ranks on top. Other large trading economies such as the United Kingdom, Germany, Korea, the United States, and Japan rank among the top 15, along with significant transhipment economies such a the United Arab Emirates, Hong-Kong (China) and Singapore.

Trade in counterfeits in container ships -- overall picture

The OECD/EUIPO study (2019) showed that virtually any economy could be the provenance of counterfeit and pirated trade. While the scope of provenance economies is broad, the raw seizures statistics also show that interceptions originate from a relatively concentrated set of provenance economies. In other words, some economies tend to dominate the global trade in counterfeit and pirated goods.

The highest number of counterfeit shipments being seized from 2014 to 2016 originated in East Asia. China and Hong-Kong (China) have been dominating global trade in counterfeit goods during the 2014-16 period, as well as during 2011-13. India, Malaysia, Mexico, Singapore, Thailand, Turkey and the United Arab Emirates remain among the top provenance economies for counterfeit and pirated goods traded worldwide within the two periods.

A review of data highlighted that while the highest number of customs seizures of counterfeit and pirated products concern postal parcels (OECD/EUIPO, 2018b), sea/vessel transport is the most concerned one in terms of seized value (Figure 4.1). Between 2014 and 2016, an average of almost 56% of the value of customs seizures of IP-infringing goods worldwide concerned sea shipments. Mail/express couriers and air transport followed, with slightly more than 19% and 16% of the value of seizures respectively. Finally, the value of seizures concerning vehicle transport amounted to about 7%. Other conveyance modes of counterfeit product, such as products carried by pedestrians or by rail, reported negligible shares.

Figure 4.1. Conveyance methods for counterfeit and pirated products, 2014-16

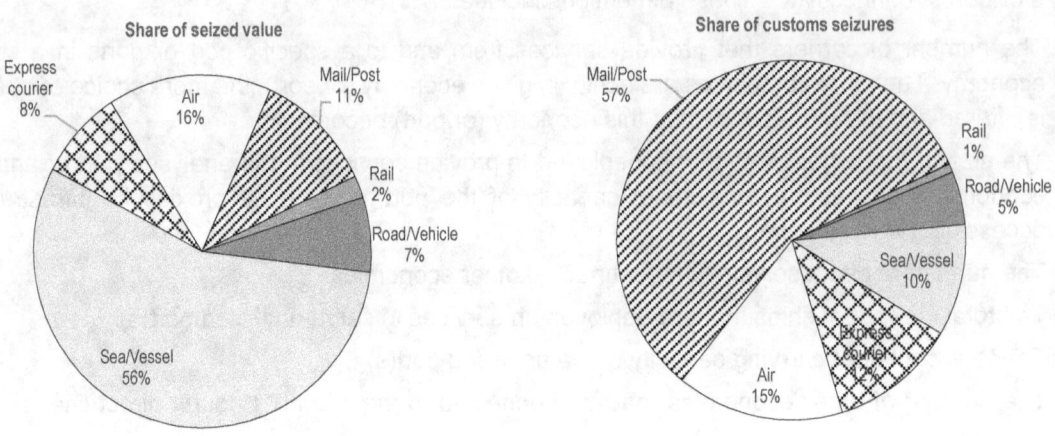

Source: OECD/EUIPO, 2019

A general, aggregated picture of the misuse of containerships in the global trade in counterfeits can be drawn based on the matching of the OECD database on customs seizures of IP-infringing products and data on the value of infrastructure investment and the volume of maritime transports provided by the OECD ITF.

Figure 4.2 indicates that the value of a provenance economy's maritime port infrastructure investment is positively correlated with the volume of its exports of fakes. Similarly, the weight of exports through maritime containers transport of a provenance economy is correlated with its value of exports in fake goods (Figure 4.3). In both figures, one point corresponds to the situation of one economy in 2016. In other words, economies with large production capacities and more developed infrastructures for handling, report higher levels of exports of counterfeit and pirated products.

Figure 4.2. Value of exports of fakes against the value of maritime port infrastructure investment by provenance economy, 2016

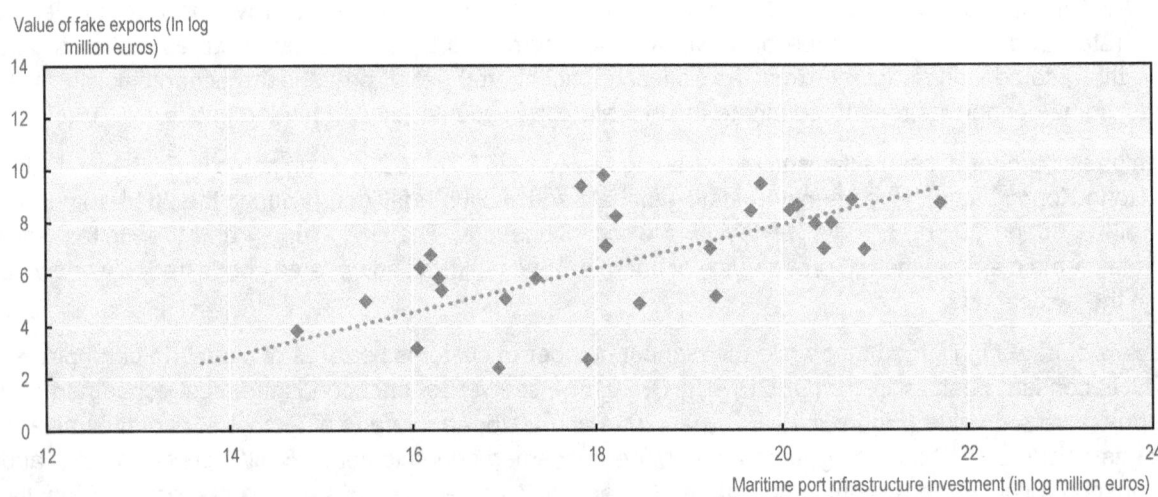

Sources: OECD database and ITF (2020).

Figure 4.3. Value of exports of fakes against the value of maritime containers transport (weight) by provenance economy. 2016.

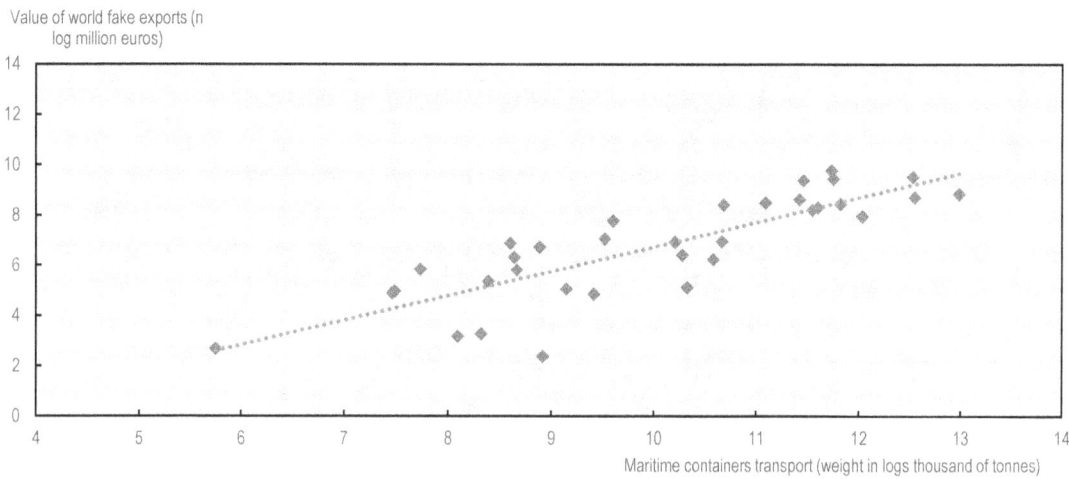

Sources: OECD database and ITF (2020).

Of course, such initial checks are likely to suffer from numerous biases. For example, these simple cross-sectional comparisons of legal and illegal dispatches by containers might be partially affected by the size of the country. This is why, a more detailed analysis based on disaggregated data by product category is needed to shed more light on the trends in counterfeit and pirated trade.

Types of fake goods more susceptible to be shipped by containers

Looking at details for the few most IP-intense and tradable product categories, [15] figures confirm that the majority of the number of global customs seizures of IP infringing goods occurred through small parcels, that is through postal or courier routes and solutions (see OECD/EUIPO,2018b) from 2014 to 2016. However, sea shipments clearly dominated in terms of the global value of fake goods seized worldwide for the large majority of them (Figure 4.4).

More specifically, Figure 4.4 below shows that, between 2014 and 2016, 82% of the seized value of counterfeit perfumes and cosmetics by customs authorities worldwide, 81% of the value of fake footwear and 73% of the value of customs seizures of fake foodstuff and toys and games concerned sea shipments. This is also the case for 58% of the global value of customs seizures of counterfeit leather articles and handbags, and 57% of fake optical, photographic and medical apparatus (including sunglasses).

Figure 4.4. Value of counterfeits seized by transports modes across selected IP-intense product categories, 2014-16

As percentage of the total value of IP-infringing goods seized worldwide by product category

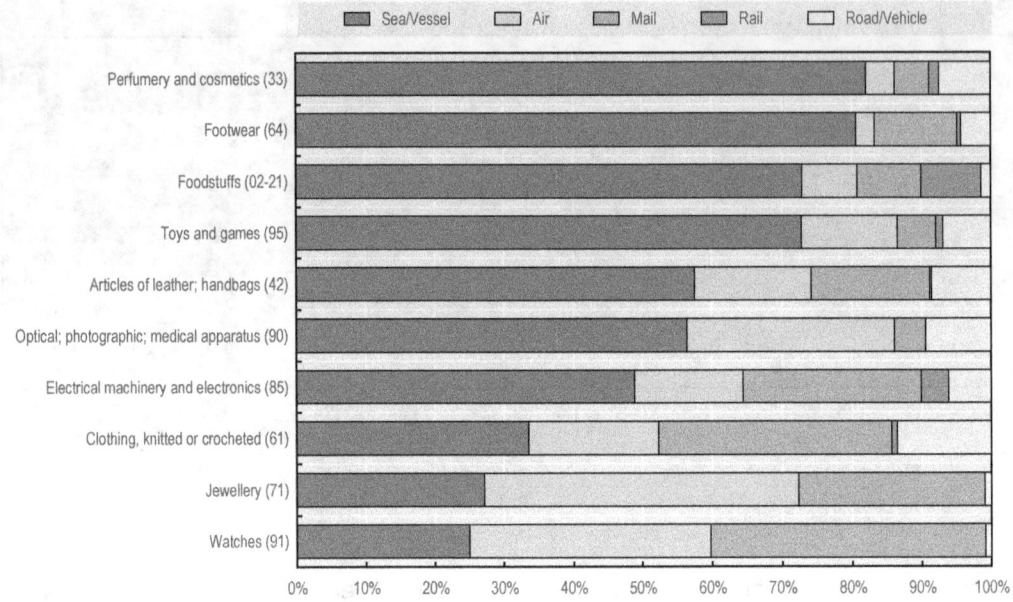

Source: OECD database

Provenance economies of containers containing fakes

The key provenance economies of seized counterfeit products shipped by sea transports are reported in Figure 4.5. The People's Republic of China appears as the largest provenance economy for container shipments, being the origin of 79% of the total value of maritime containers containing fakes seized worldwide. It is followed by India (5%), Far East Asian economies (Malaysia, Viet Nam and Pakistan, 3.6% in total), the United Arab Emirates (1.4%), Turkey (0.8%), Hong Kong (China) and Chinese Taipei (0.7% each) and North African economies, such as Morocco and Egypt (0.5% each).

Figure 4.5. Top 10 provenance economies in the value seized maritime containers transporting counterfeits, 2014-16

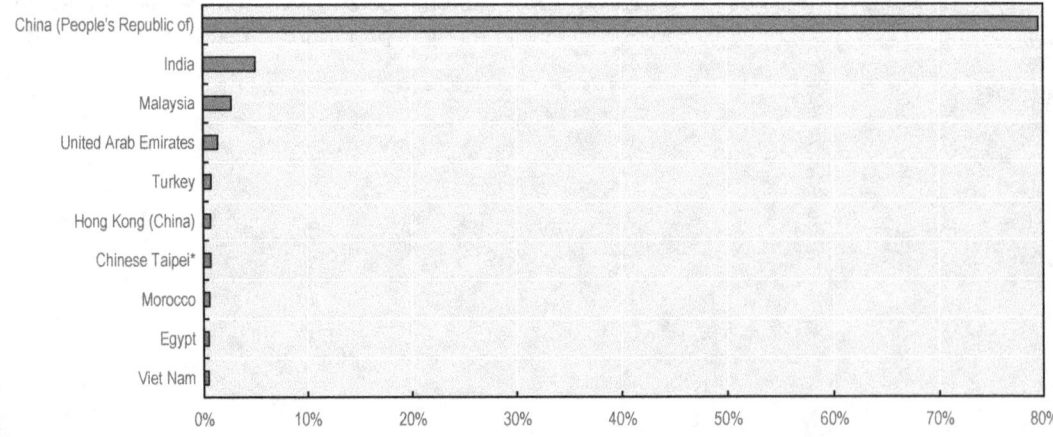

Source: OECD database

Figure 4.6 presents the ratio of percentage of container seizures in a given economy to the average percentage of containers seizures across the top 20 provenance economies.[16] This ratio shows the relative intensity of exports of fakes in containers from key provenance economies, as opposed to other potential modes of transport. The results indicate that in some economies criminals are more likely to misuse maritime transport for exporting counterfeit goods. The countries where the ratio is particularly high are the Djibouti, Cambodia, Morocco, India, and China, respectively. For instance, in Djibouti and Cambodia, the seizures by containers are almost 2.1 and 1.9 times higher than on average.

Figure 4.6. Economies most likely to use containers for exporting fake goods among the top 20 provenance economies in terms of their propensity to export counterfeit goods (GTRIC-e, average 2014-16)

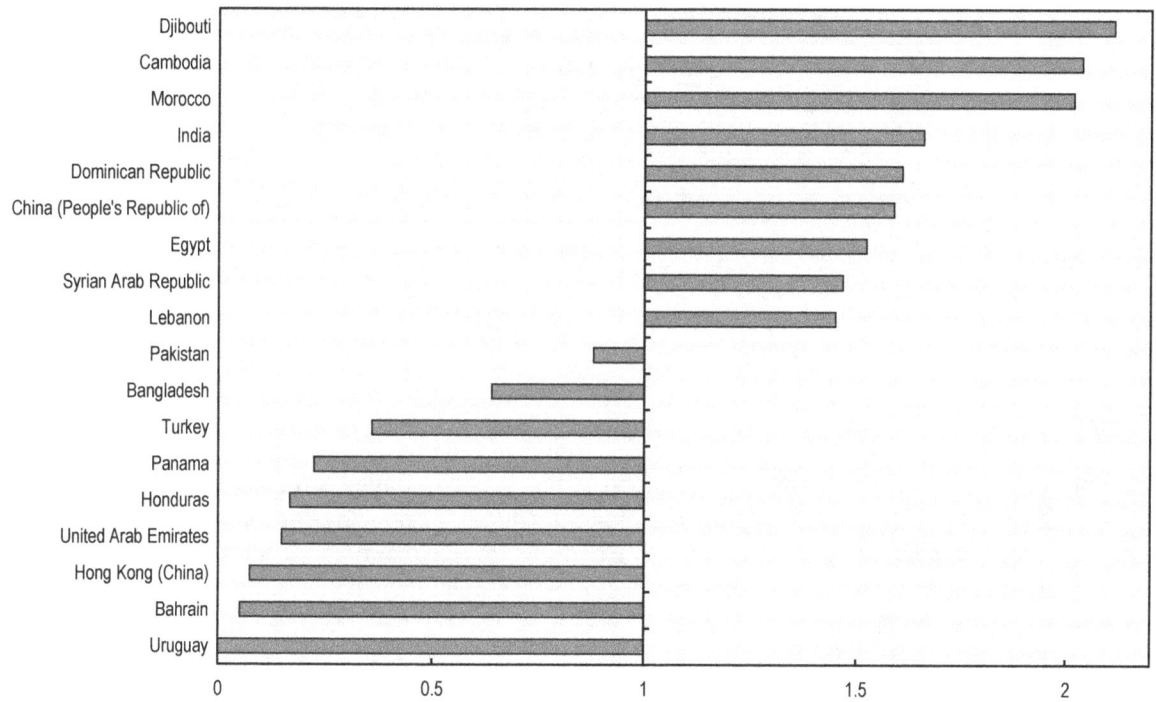

Source: OECD database

Figure 4.7 lists the transport modes used by top provenance economies for exporting fake goods. In some provenance economies, like Morocco or Djibouti, containers are the preferred mode for exporting counterfeit products. In India and China, around 78% and 75% of the value of export counterfeit goods is sent by sea. However, in other provenance economies, e.g. Hong Kong (China), the share of export of fakes by the containers is relatively low (equal to 5%) and postal shipments are the preferred mode for exporting fake goods.

Figure 4.7. Share of the value of fake exports by transport mode for the top 20 provenance economies of fake goods in terms of GTRIC-e (average 2014-16)

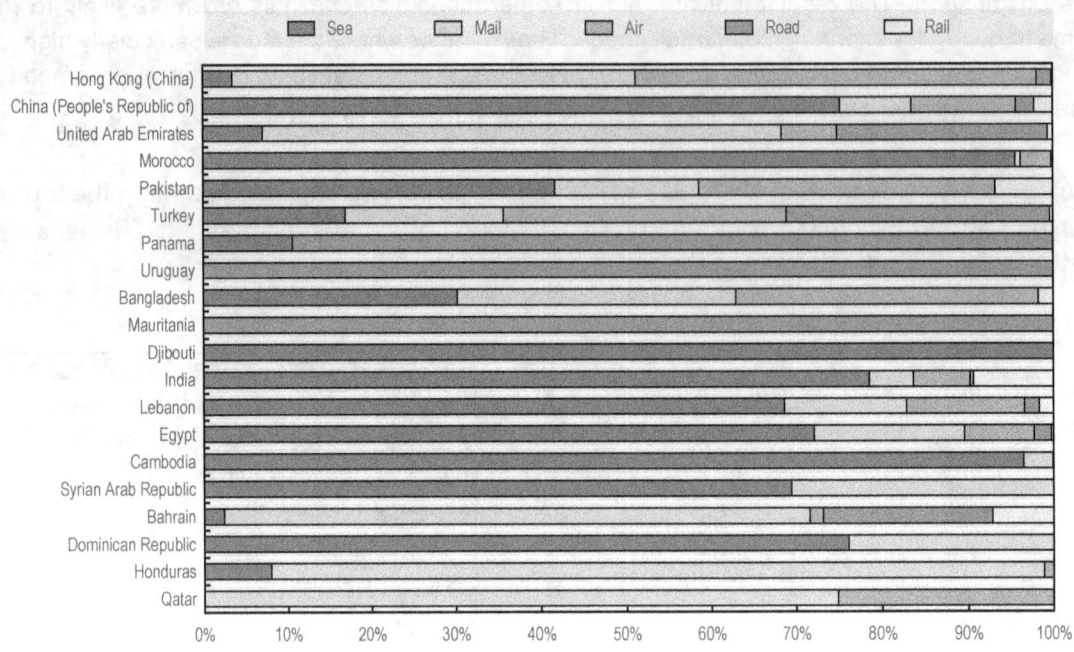

Source: OECD database

Industry-specific analysis

Regarding industry-specific patterns, as described in the section above, container ships are commonly used by counterfeiters in many industry sectors prone to counterfeiting. However, there are some product categories where counterfeiting is a particularly big problem. For example, in terms of value, for many industry sectors including perfumery and cosmetics; articles of leather; toys and games, value of seized fakes smuggled with containerships exceeded 50% of total value of seizures (see figure 4.4. above). This subsection looks more specifically at those sectors that seem to suffer the most from counterfeiting, involving the misuse of containerships. The analysis is carried out in sectors where data of sufficient quality are available. These sectors include: perfumery and cosmetics; leather articles; clothing, electronics and electrical equipment; toys and games. The total value of counterfeits smuggled with containers, as a proportion of the total value of illicit trade in fakes in these sectors, ranged between 35% (clothing) and almost 85% (perfumery and cosmetics).

The main source of data for the industry-specific analysis of major provenance countries is the OECD database of counterfeit seizures. Usually, each seizure indicates the provenance country which may be either the country where the counterfeit product has been produced or the last country of its departure, if custom authorities are not able to establish the origin of the counterfeit good. This poses some important limitations that make it difficult to distinguish between producers and transhipment countries and reconstruct major trade routes of counterfeit products. The UNIDO INDSTAT database has been used as an additional data source to verify legitimate productive capacity of the major provenance countries of the counterfeit goods in each product category.

Both, the absolute output of legitimate products and revealed comparative advantage indicators (RCAP-e) in the production in each product category for the major provenance countries have been analysed to ascribe most probable role of each country in the trade of counterfeit products.[17]

The detailed findings of the analysis are presented in the subsections below, while Table 4.1 summarizes the key findings.

Table 4.1. Key producers and transit points in illicit trade in fakes in containerships, in five main targeted industries (2016)

Industry	Identified potential producers of fakes trades with containerships	Identified potential transit points in illicit trade in fakes with containerships
Perfumery and cosmetics	China, India, Malaysia	United Arab Emirates
Leather articles and handbags	China, Malaysia, Morocco, Thailand, India, Turkey	Hong Kong [China]; United Arab Emirates
Clothing	China, Malaysia, India	Hong Kong [China]; United Arab Emirates
Electronics and electrical equipment	China, Malaysia	Hong Kong [China]; United Arab Emirates; Malaysia
Toys and games	China, Malaysia, India	Hong Kong [China]; United Arab Emirates; Singapore

Note: Data source: Eurostat table mar_go_qm_c2016 Volume of containers transported to/from main ports. Table 4.31 presents inward flow of total number of containers (loaded and empty) from five major counterfeit provenance countries: China, Hong Kong (China), Singapore, United Arab Emirates and Turkey. For the table quarterly data has been aggregated to annual figures.
Source: Authors' calculations based on OECD database.

The results highlight that for all five analysed sectors, China is the main producer of fakes that are then transported with containerships; Malaysia and India play minor roles. In addition, Turkey also plays some role, especially when it comes to production destined for the EU markets.

The networks of global liner operators are based on traffic circulation through strategic transhipment hubs, which play a crucial role in the extensive hub-feeder container system. Singapore and Hong-Kong (China) play important roles in this system, accounting for 50 per cent of all ports activity in 2006, up from 39 per cent ten years earlier (Ducruet and Notteboom, 2012)

Perfumery and cosmetics

Overview

The perfumery and cosmetics industry refers to products in the HS 33 product category. Over the period 2014-2016, there are various examples of counterfeit perfumery and cosmetics recorded in the OECD database of customs seizures, such as counterfeit make-up, creams, aftershaves, shampoos, luxury perfumes, nail sets, and even toothpaste and toothbrushes. In some cases, these counterfeit products are unsafe and can thus pose a serious health threat to consumers.

According to calculations in the OECD-EUIPO (2019) study, global trade in counterfeit perfumery and cosmetics was valued at up to USD 5.3 billion (EUR 4.9 billion) in 2016. This represents 4.7% of global trade in perfumes and cosmetics, placing the industry in the top 15 most affected by global counterfeiting and piracy in terms of value.

The analysis of the value of customs seizures reflects that the value of shipments made by sea was by far the largest as compared to others shipment modes (82%, Figure 4.8, right panel). In terms of the number of customs seizures, the largest share of shipments of counterfeit perfumery and cosmetics was by mail, accounting for 60% of the total number of global customs seizures of infringing perfumes and cosmetic preparations (Figure 4.8, left panel). Containers ranked third (15%), just behind road transport (16%).

Figure 4.8. Shipment methods for seized counterfeit perfumes and cosmetics, 2014-2016

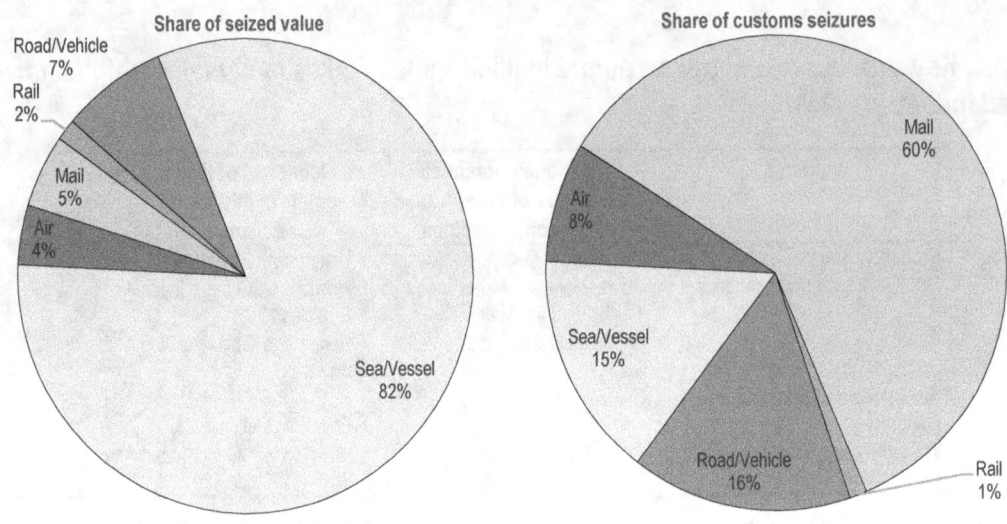

Source: OECD database

The People's Republic of China, Malaysia, the United Arab Emirates are the most important sources of counterfeit perfumery and cosmetics seized worldwide and shipped by containers (Figure 4.9). However, the People's Republic of China clearly dominates, being the source of 84% of fake perfumes and cosmetics exported throughout the world by containers.

Analysis of the productive capacity of the major provenance economies of counterfeit perfumes and cosmetics indicates that China, India and Malaysia may be the major producers of the counterfeit products, while the United Arab Emirates is the major transhipment hub through which those products are shipped to final destinations.

Figure 4.9. Provenance economies of seized containers containing perfumes and cosmetics, 2014-16

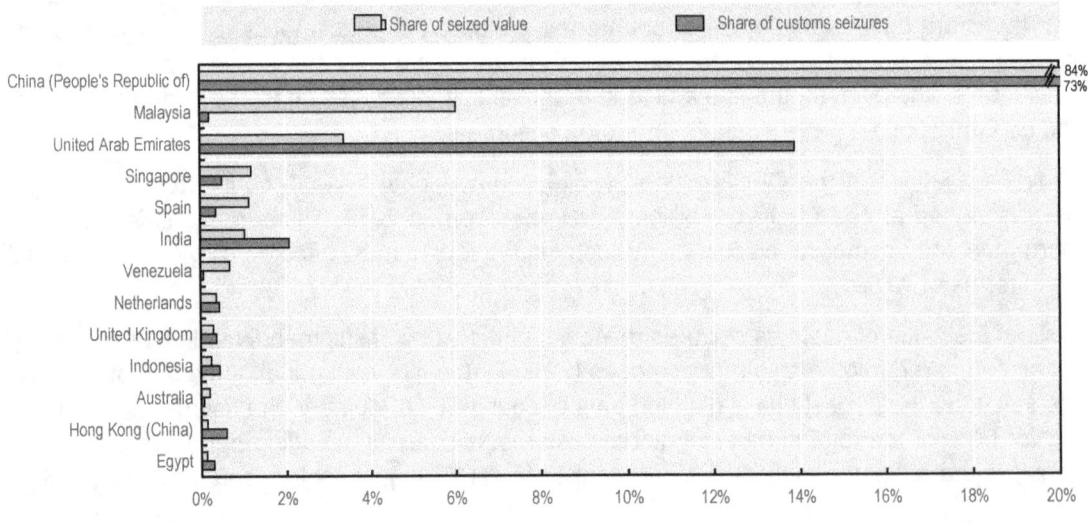

Source: OECD database

Cross features

The legal flows of perfumes and cosmetics exported from a given provenance economy by containers can be compared with the value of fake perfumes and cosmetics shipped from that economy.

Figure 4.10 and Figure 4.11 plot the quantity of total exports of perfumes and cosmetics shipped from each extra-EU provenance economy to each EU member state by containers in 2016 against the value of counterfeit and pirated goods shipped from/to the same economies by (i) all transport modes confounded, (ii) only sea shipments, respectively.

Both exercises result in positive correlations that in both cases are statistically significant. It means that in general all trade flows in cosmetics and perfumes are to some degree "polluted" with counterfeit goods.

Figure 4.10. Counterfeit perfumes and cosmetics: quantity of total exports by containers against total value of seizures of fake goods, 2016

By each EU destination economy and extra-EU provenance economy pair

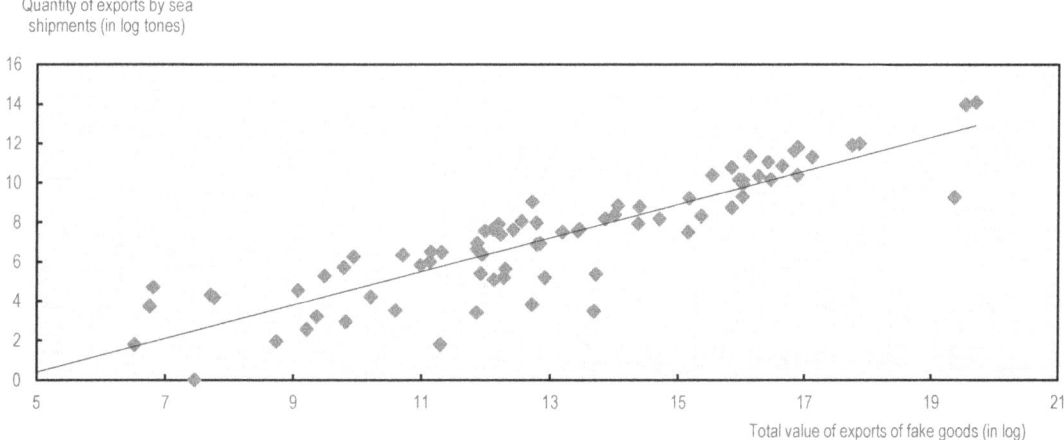

Note: One point corresponds to the flow of exports from a single provenance economy to a single EU destination economy in 2016.
Sources: OECD database and Comext (2020).

Figure 4.11. Counterfeit perfumes and cosmetics: quantity of legal exports by containers against value of seizures of fake goods by containers, 2016

For each EU destination economy and extra-EU provenance economy pair

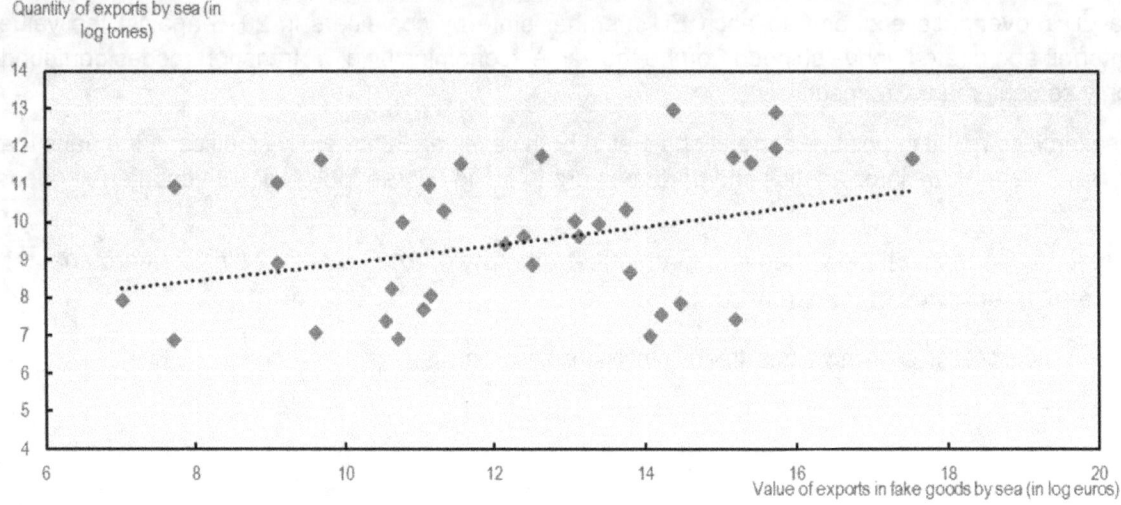

Note: One point corresponds to the flow of exports from a single provenance economy to a single EU destination economy in 2016.
Sources: OECD database and Comext (2020).

Leather articles and handbags

Overview

The leather articles and handbag industry refers to products in the HS 42 product category. This category notably includes articles of apparel and footwear accessories made of leather or of composition leather as well as trunks, suits, cameras, jewellery, cutlery cases, travel, tool and similar bags wholly or mainly covered by leather, composition leather, plastic sheeting or textile materials.

According to calculations for the OECD-EUIPO (2019) study, global trade in counterfeit articles of leather and handbags was up to USD 8.5 billion (EUR 7.7 billion) in 2016. This represents more than 12.3% of the total trade in leather articles and handbags and makes the industry the second most affected by global counterfeiting and piracy in terms of trade percentage (after footwear, see next subsection).

Over the period 2014-16, the largest share of the value of seized shipments of counterfeit articles of leather and handbags was sent by containers (57%, Figure 4.12, left panel). This is the case even if postal shipments dominate in terms of the number of seizures (79%, Figure 4.12, right panel).

Figure 4.12. Shipment methods for seized counterfeit articles of leather and handbags, 2011-13

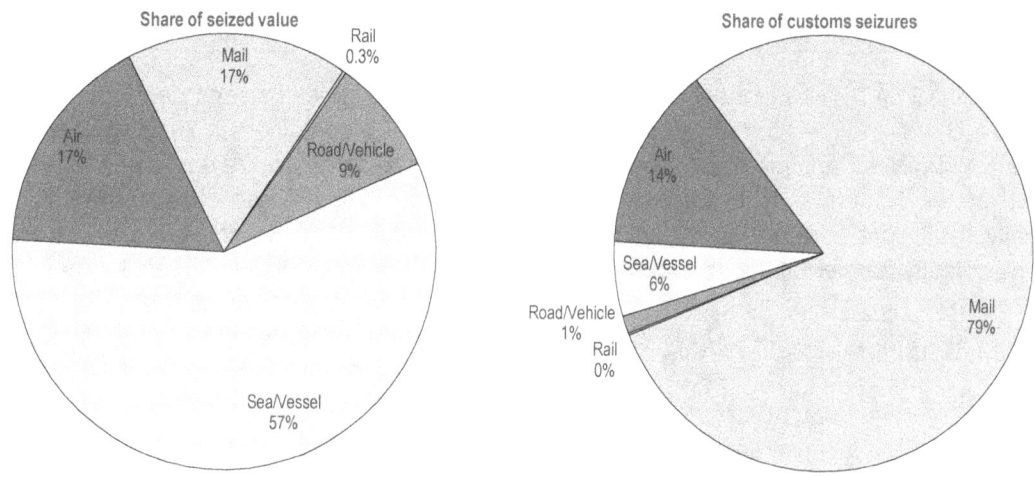

Source: OECD database

China was the main source of counterfeit leather articles and handbags shipped worldwide by sea shipments. It was followed by the United Arab Emirates, Malaysia, Hong Kong (China), Morocco, Thailand, India, and Turkey, respectively (Figure 4.13).

Analysis of the productive capacity of the major provenance economies of leather articles indicates that China is a major producer of counterfeit leather articles, with Malaysia, Morocco, Thailand, India and Turkey playing also some role in the production of leather counterfeit goods. United Arab Emirates and Hong Kong (China) are the most important transhipment hubs of leather products.

Figure 4.13. Top provenance economies of sea shipments containing counterfeit leather articles and handbags, 2014-16

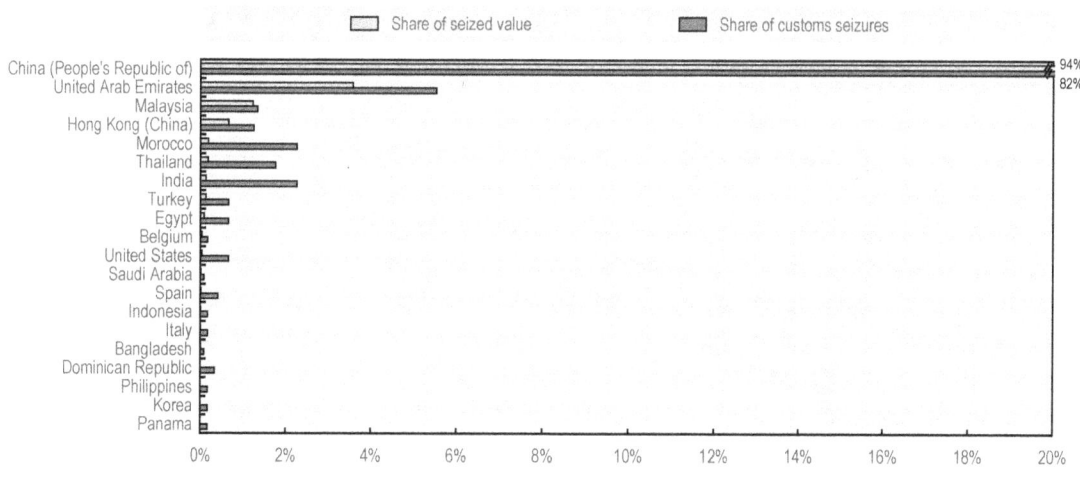

Source: OECD database

Cross features

The legal flows of articles of leather and handbags exported from a given economy by containers can be compared with the value of fake leather articles and handbags shipped from that economy.

Figure 4.14 and Figure 4.15 plot the quantity of genuine articles of leather and handbags shipped from each extra-EU provenance economy to each EU member state by containers in 2016 against the value of counterfeit and pirated articles of leather and handbags shipped from/to the same economies by (i) all transport modes confounded, (ii) only sea shipments, respectively. These checks show positive and statistically significant correlations. It indicates that on average all trade flows in leather articles and handbags contain counterfeit goods. Counterfeiting is a universal threat to all markets for these products.

Figure 4.14. Counterfeit leather articles and handbags: quantity of legal exports by containers against total value of seizures of fake goods, 2016

By each EU destination economy and extra-EU provenance economy pair

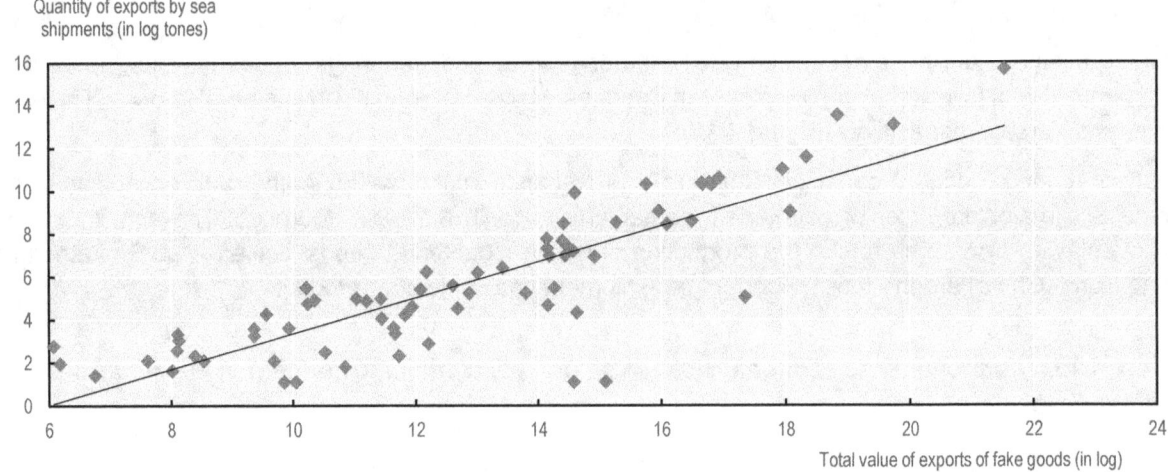

Note: One point corresponds to the flow of exports from a single provenance economy to a single EU destination economy in 2016.
Sources: OECD database and Comext (2020).

Figure 4.15. Counterfeit leather articles and handbags: quantity of legal exports by containers against value of seizures of fake goods by containers, 2016

By each EU destination economy and extra-EU provenance economy pair

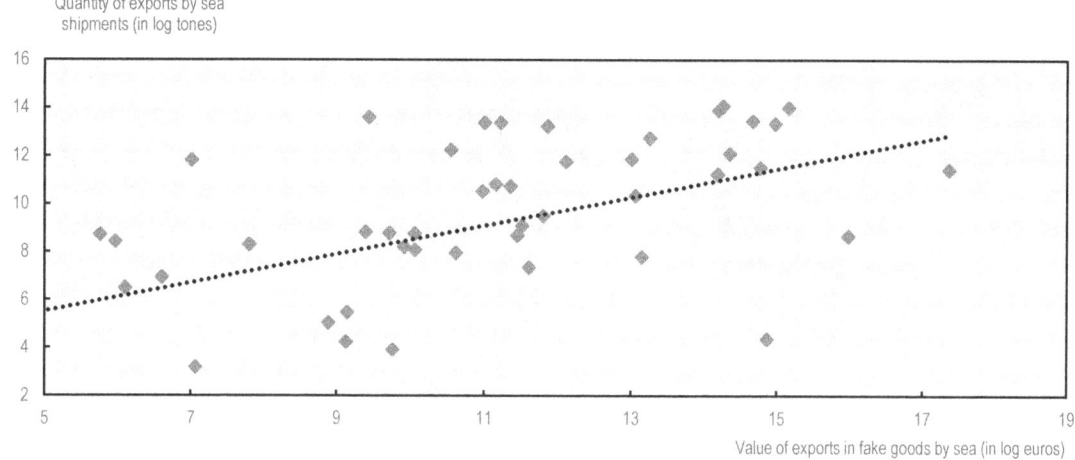

Note: One point corresponds to the flow of exports from a single provenance economy to a single EU destination economy in 2016.
Sources: OECD database and Comext (2020).

Clothing

Overview

The clothing industry refers to products in the HS 61 product category, and mainly includes shirts, blouses, coats and suits.

According to calculations for the OECD-EUIPO (2019) study, global trade in counterfeit clothing was up to USD 24.8 billion (EUR 22.5 billion) in 2016. This represents more than 13.1% of global trade in footwear and ranks the industry as the most significant one affected by global counterfeiting and piracy in relative terms (i.e. as a percentage of world imports within the product category) and fourth in terms of value.

The analysis of the value of customs seizures reflects that the value of shipments made by sea was the largest in the total value of shipments of IP-infringing clothing (33%, Figure 4.16, left panel). However, most of seizures of counterfeit clothing were effectuated while goods were transported by mail (63%, Figure 4.16, right panel). Smaller shares went by air (19%), road (10%) and sea (8%).

Figure 4.16. Shipment methods for seized counterfeit clothing and textile fabrics, 2011-13

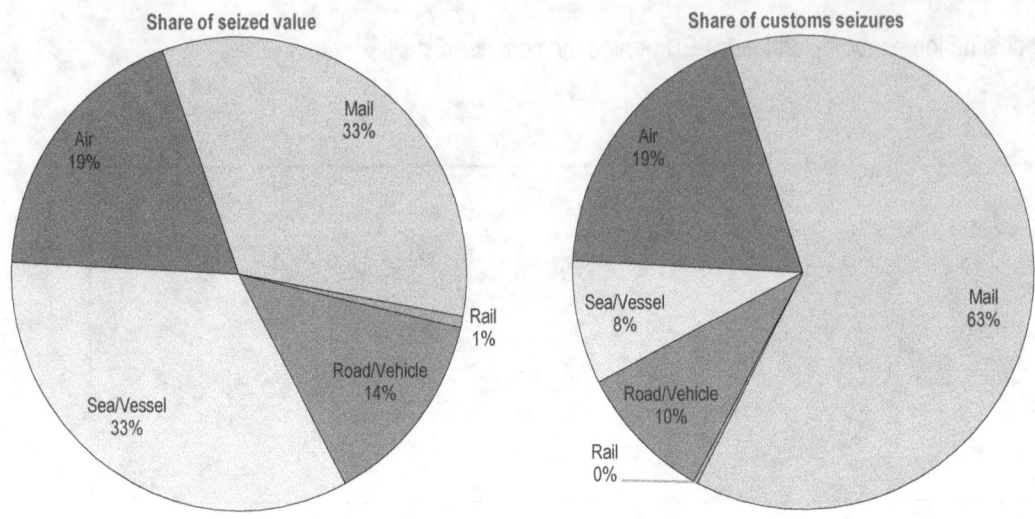

The People's Republic of China is the main producer and exporter of counterfeit clothing shipped by sea, followed by Malaysia and India. Then come Hong Kong (China), Bangladesh, Morocco, Indonesia, the United Arab Emirates and Morocco. All those countries have important productive capacity as regards clothing so they may be the source of production of counterfeit clothing goods. Hong Kong (China), United Arab Emirates and Malaysia may be also important as transhipment hubs for counterfeit clothing goods as well.

Figure 4.17. Provenance economies of seized containers containing counterfeit clothes, 2014-16

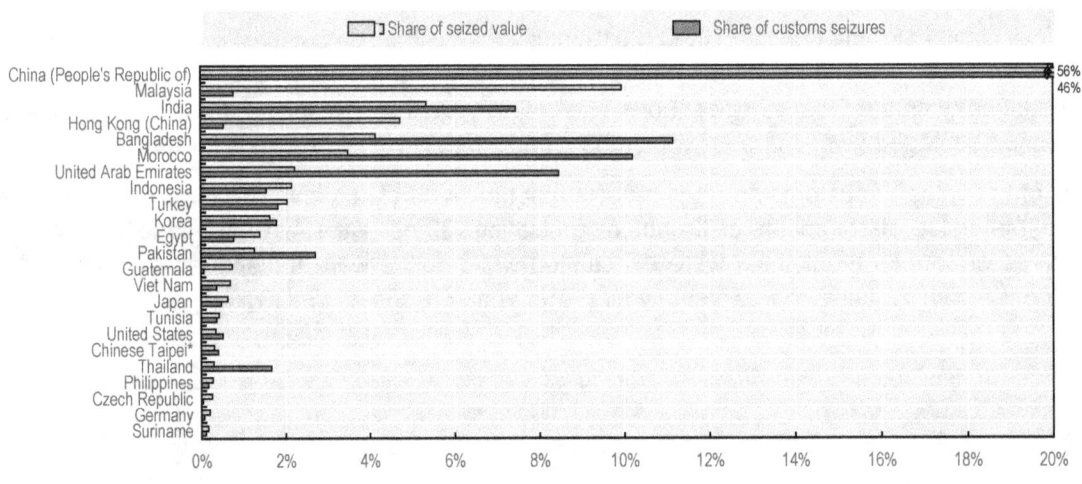

Source: OECD database

Cross features

The legal flows of clothing exported from a given economy by containers can be compared with the value of fake clothing shipped from that economy.

Figure 4.18 and Figure 4.19 plot the quantity of clothing shipped from each extra-EU provenance economy to each EU member state by containers in 2016 against the value of counterfeit and pirated clothing shipped from/to the same economies by (i) all transport modes confounded, (ii) only sea shipments, respectively. In both cases correlations are positive and statistically significant. It shows that on average any trade route where containers are used to transport these goods becomes targeted by criminals.

Figure 4.18. Counterfeit clothing: quantity of legal exports by containers against total value of seizures of fake goods, 2016

By each EU destination economy and extra-EU provenance economy pair

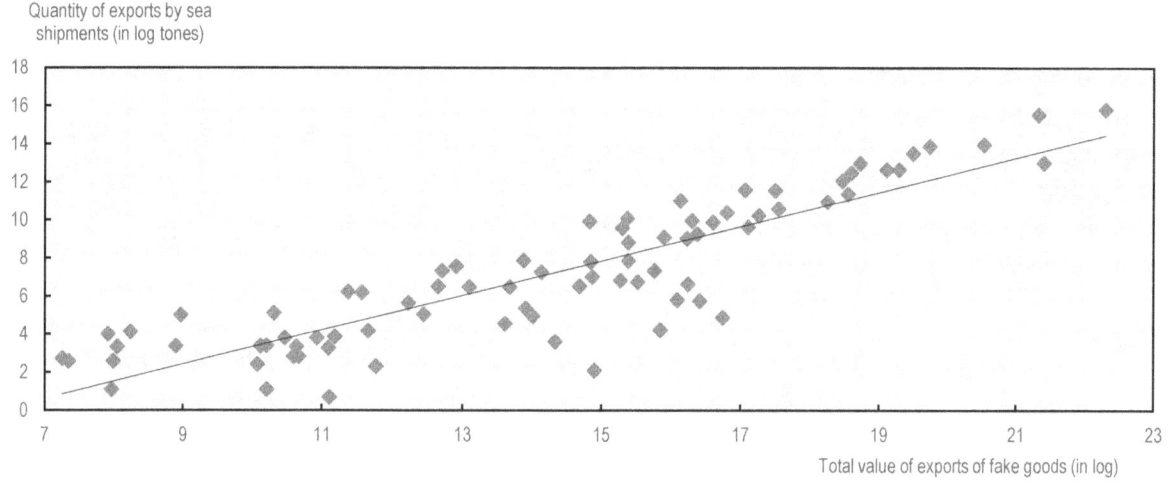

Note: One point corresponds to the flow of exports from a single provenance economy to a single EU destination economy in 2016.
Sources: OECD database and Comext (2020).

Figure 4.19. Counterfeit clothing: quantity of legal exports by containers against value of seizures of fake goods by containers, 2016

By each EU destination economy and extra-EU provenance economy pair

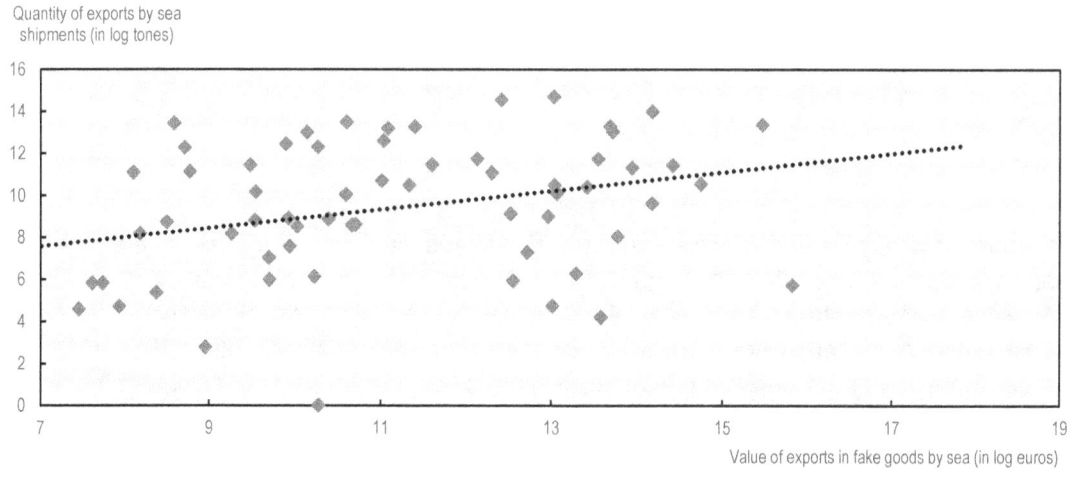

Note: One point corresponds to the flow of exports from a single provenance economy to a single EU destination economy in 2016.
Sources: OECD database and Comext (2020).

Electronic and electrical equipment

Overview

Electronic and electrical equipment industry refers to products in the HS 85 product category. Over the period 2014-16, customs authorities worldwide notably recorded seizures of counterfeit memory cards and sticks, earphones, headphones and headsets, mobile phones, batteries, chargers, microphones, speakers, and even electronic integrated circuits.

According to calculations for the OECD-EUIPO (2019) study, global trade in counterfeit electronic devices and electrical equipment was valued at USD 138 billion (EUR 125 billion) in 2016, making this industry the most affected by global counterfeiting and piracy in terms of value. This represents more than 5.6% of the total trade in those products.

Over the period 2014-16, the analysis of the value of customs seizures reflects that the size of shipments made by sea (49%, Figure 4.20, left panel) was larger than the size of shipments of fake electronics and electrical equipment made by mail. In terms of number, the largest share of seizures of counterfeit electronics and electrical equipment was sent by mail, representing 64% of all global customs seizures of these products reported in the database (Figure 4.20, right panel).

Figure 4.20. Shipment methods for seized counterfeit electronics and electrical equipment, 2014-16

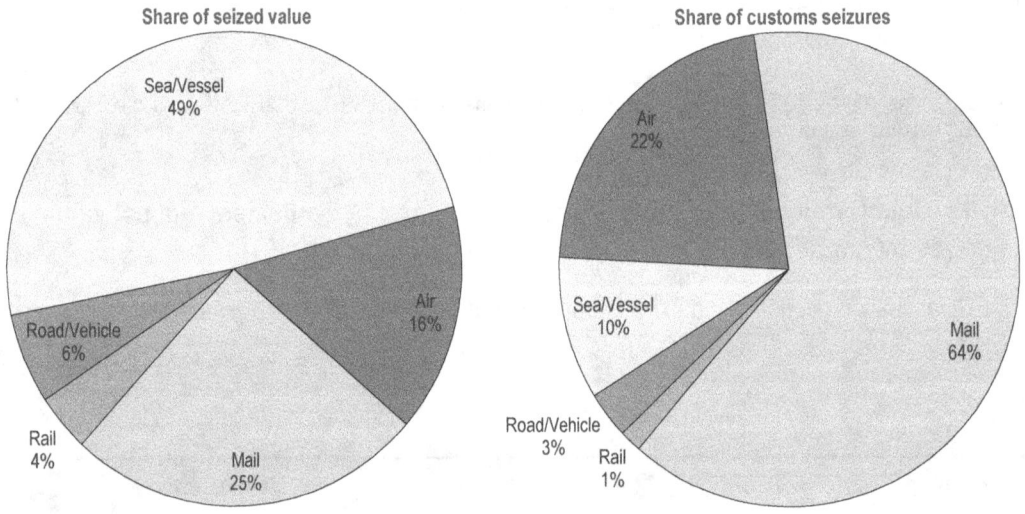

Source: OECD database

The People's Republic of China and Malaysia are the main producers of counterfeit electronics and electrical equipment shipped by containers (Figure 4.21). Seizures data indicate complex trade routes used by counterfeiters of the electronic and electrical products with some highly developed countries being used as a transhipment/producer of products in HS 85 seized in developing countries. Nevertheless, the United Arab Emirates and Hong-Kong (China) seem to be the major transhipment hubs for counterfeiting electronic goods shipped to the final destinations.

Figure 4.21. Provenance economies of containers containing counterfeit electronics and electrical equipment, 2014-16

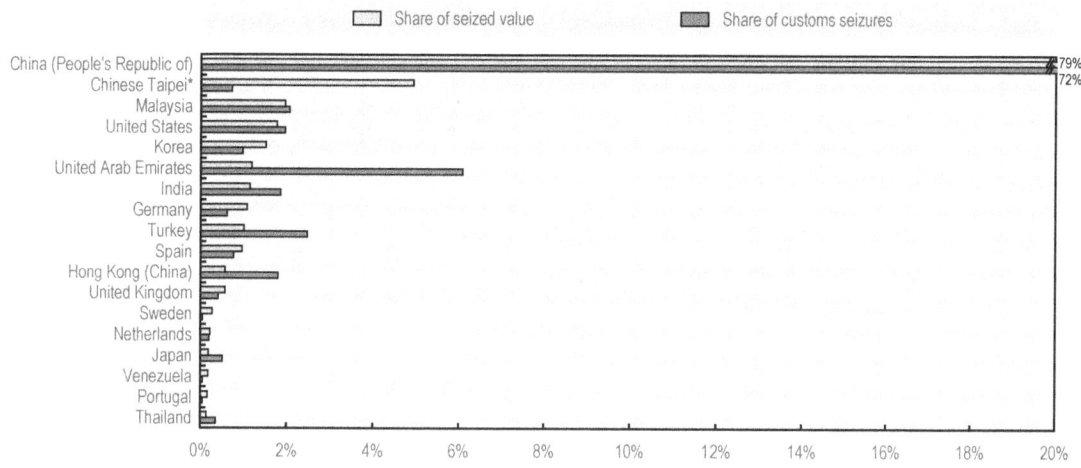

Source: OECD database

Cross features

The legal flows of electronic and electrical goods exported from a given economy by containers can be compared with the value of fake electronic and electrical goods shipped from that economy.

Figure 4.22 and Figure 4.23 plot the quantity of genuine electronic and electrical goods shipped from each extra-EU provenance economy to each EU member state by containers in 2016 against the value of counterfeit and pirated electronic and electrical goods shipped from/to the same economies by (i) all transport modes confounded, (ii) only sea shipments, respectively. Both correlations are positive and significant. It indicates that to some extent all trade flows in electronic and electrical equipment are polluted with counterfeit goods, making counterfeiting is a genera threat to this sector of the industry.

Figure 4.22. Counterfeit electronics and electrical goods: quantity of legal exports by containers against total value of seizures of fake goods, 2016

By each EU destination economy and extra-EU provenance economy pair

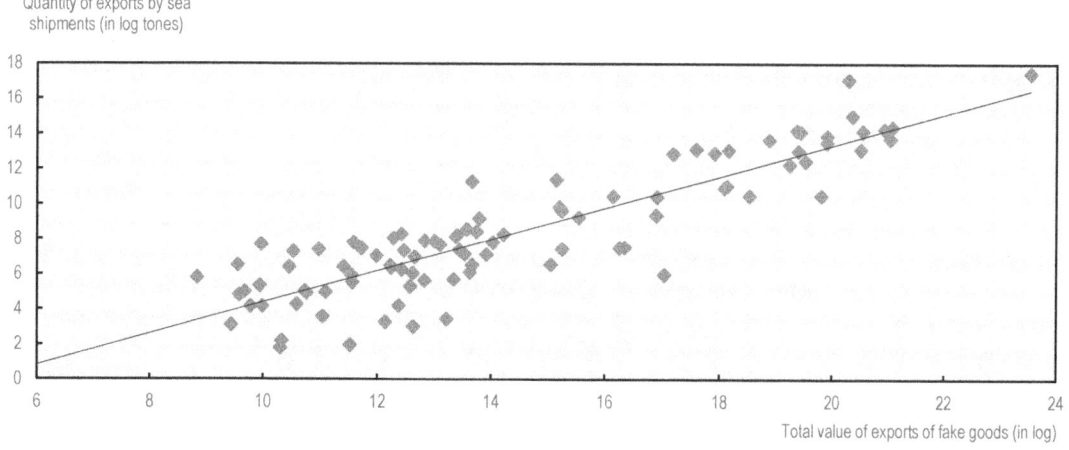

Note: One point corresponds to the flow of exports from a single provenance economy to a single EU destination economy in 2016.
Sources: OECD database and Comext (2020).

Figure 4.23. Counterfeit electronics and electrical equipment; quantity of legal exports by containers against value of seizures of fake goods by containers, 2016

By each EU destination economy and extra-EU provenance economy pair

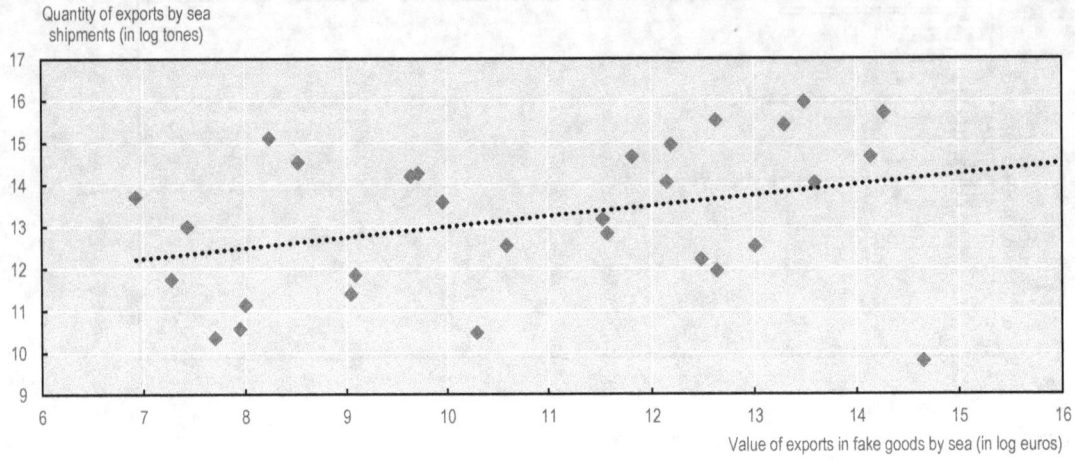

Note: One point corresponds to the flow of exports from a single provenance economy to a single EU destination economy in 2016.
Sources: OECD database and Comext (2020).

Toys and games

Overview

The toys, games and sports equipment industry refers to products in the HS 95 product category. Over the period 2014-16, customs authorities worldwide mainly seized counterfeit video game consoles and controllers, balls and balloons, bicycles, boxing gloves, car models, cards, exercise equipment, figures, plastic toys, skateboards, robots and dolls.

According to calculations for the OECD-EUIPO (2019) study, global trade in counterfeit toys, games and sports equipment was worth USD 11.8 billion (EUR 10.7 billion) in 2016. This represented more than 11.2% of all trade in those products, making this industry the third most affected by global counterfeiting and piracy in relative terms (i.e. as a percentage of trade within the product category).

Over the period 2014-16, the largest share of the global value of customs seizures of fake toys and games was made by sea (73%, Figure 4.24, left panel). Sea shipments were also close to the top in terms of the number of customs seizures of counterfeit toys and games traded worldwide, just slightly behind postal shipments (39% and 41%, Figure 4.24, right panel).

Figure 4.24. Shipment methods for seized counterfeit toys and games, 2014-16

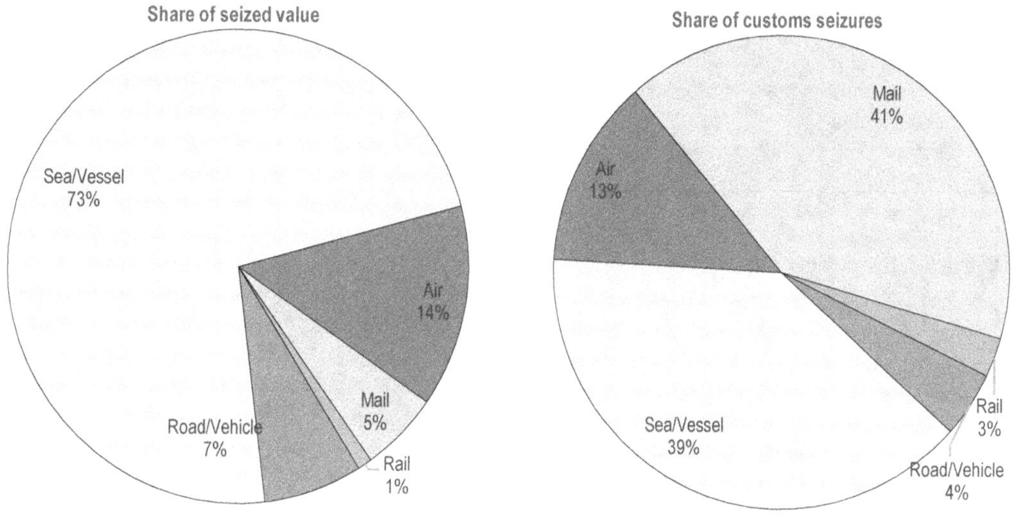

Share of seized value
- Sea/Vessel 73%
- Air 14%
- Road/Vehicle 7%
- Mail 5%
- Rail 1%

Share of customs seizures
- Mail 41%
- Sea/Vessel 39%
- Air 13%
- Road/Vehicle 4%
- Rail 3%

Source: OECD database.

The People's Republic of China, Malaysia and India appear to be the main producing economies exporting fake toys, games and sports equipment by containers. The United Arab Emirates, Hong Kong (China) and Singapore are indicated as the main transit points for counterfeit toys, games and sports equipment worldwide.

Cross features

The legal flows of toys and games exported from a given economy by containers can be compared with the value of fake toys and games shipped from that economy.

Figure 4.25 and Figure 4.26 plot the quantity of genuine toys and games shipped from each extra-EU provenance economy to each EU member state by containers in 2016 against the value of counterfeit and pirated toys and games shipped from/to the same economies by (i) all transport modes, (ii) only sea shipments, respectively. Just as for previous industries analysed in this report the correlations are positive and statistically significant. It means that on average all trade flows in toys become targeted by criminals, making counterfeiting a general, universal threat to this industry.

Figure 4.25. Counterfeit toys and games: quantity of legal exports by containers against total value of seizures of fake goods, 2016

By each EU destination economy and extra-EU provenance economy pair

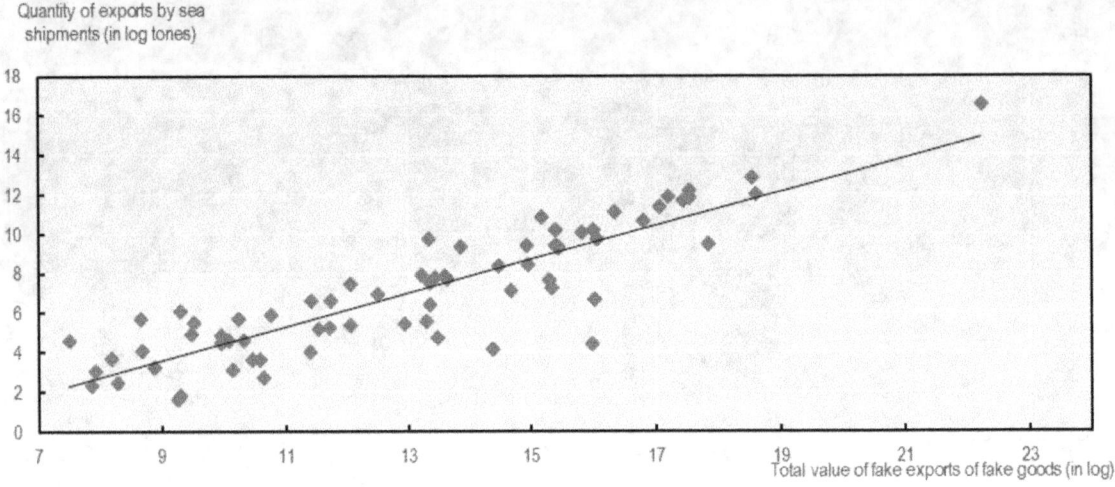

Note: One point corresponds to the flow of exports from a single provenance economy to a single EU destination economy in 2016.
Sources: OECD database and Comext (2020).

Figure 4.26. Counterfeit toys and games: quantity of legal exports by containers against total value of seizures of fake goods by containers, 2016

By each EU destination economy and extra-EU provenance economy pair

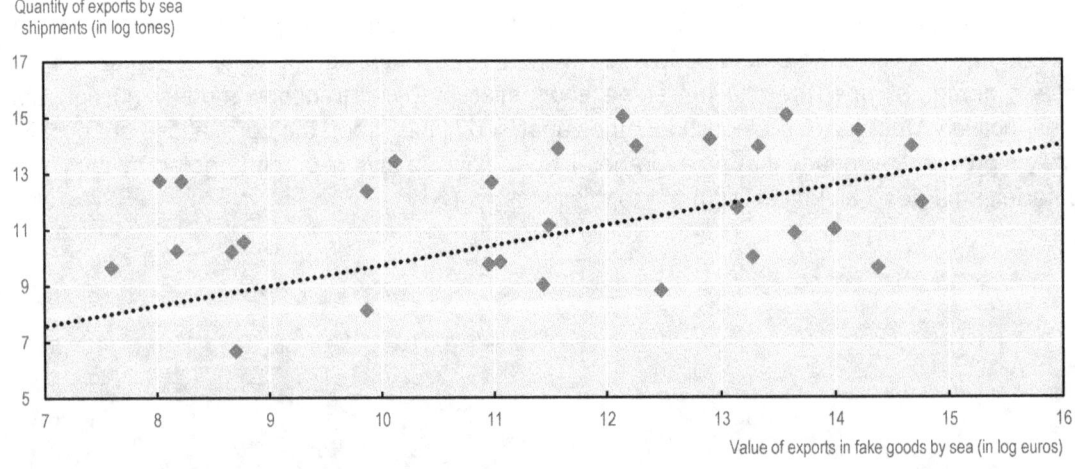

Note: One point corresponds to the flow of exports from a single provenance economy to a single EU destination economy in 2016.
Sources: OECD database and Comext (2020).

Key maritime routes for illicit trade

The general analysis presented above documents the scale of misuse of containerized maritime transport in illicit trade in counterfeits. It estimates its scale, identifies key provenance economies, illustrates products concerned and gauges this phenomenon for key industries concerned.

The analysis provides additional evidence of the role of containerized maritime transport in counterfeit trade. The analysis builds on findings presented in the OECD-EUIPO (2018c) report that assessed the role of governance frameworks, enforcement and economic factors in relation to intensity of trade in fake goods. The analysis is done in three steps:

- First, this section reiterates some of the points made in the OECD-EUIPO (2018c) report in the context of container containerized maritime transport. It starts with a general check of some links between the share of counterfeit and pirated goods exported by each economy and general indicators on its logistic facilities.
- In addition, the analysis identifies the key shipping container routes that tend to be polluted with counterfeits. This question is analysed specifically for the routes for the EU, where detailed data are available.
- To conclude, this subchapter also discusses potential changes in these patterns in the context of future infrastructural and logistical developments.

To check whether the problem of misuse of counterfeits follows the general patterns of illicit trade in fakes, as outlined in OECD-EUIPO (2018c), this section analyses the relation between illicit trade in counterfeits and maritime trade flows in general. This section presents it using three general, aggregated indices that illustrate the accessibility of containerized trade in a given economy, developed by UNCTAD. These measures reflect the degree of integration of an economy and its ports in global trade, hence they constitute a proxy for the general level of development of an economy infrastructure and its openness. These indices include:

- Port liner shipping connectivity index, an aggregated indicator of relative importance and integration of a port in global trade. This section checks its relation with the value of imports of fakes sezied by customs in a given economy (see Figure 4.27).
- Liners Shipping bilateral connectivity index (UNCTAD), which indicates a country pair's integration level into global liner shipping networks. This index is aggregated and averaged for exporting economies and then it is compared with the corresponding value of exports of fake goods by sea from this economy (see Figure 4.28).
- Container port traffic index, that measures the flow of containers from land to sea transport modes., and vice versa, in twenty-foot equivalent units (TEUs) a standard-size container. Its relation is checked with the value of imports of fakes seized by customs in a given economy (see Figure 4.29).

The Liner Shipping Connectivity Index (LSCI) aims at capturing the level of integration into the existing liner shipping network by measuring liner shipping connectivity. It can be calculated at the country and at the port level. LSCI can be considered a proxy of the accessibility to global trade.

In all three cases there is strong, and statistically significant correlation between indices of trade in counterfeit goods misusing containerized maritime transport and indices of intensity of containerized maritime transport in general.

A conclusion of this exercise is that illicit trade in counterfeits that misuses maritime transport is a universal and general problem, which correlates with the openness and development of an economy shipping lines infrastructure. Put it differently, similarly to findings of OECD-EUIPO (2018c) illicit trade in counterfeits tends to correlate with indices of an economy's openness, and integration in global trade.

Figure 4.27. Correlation between the Port LSCI index and proxy for trade in counterfeits. Economy-level, 2016

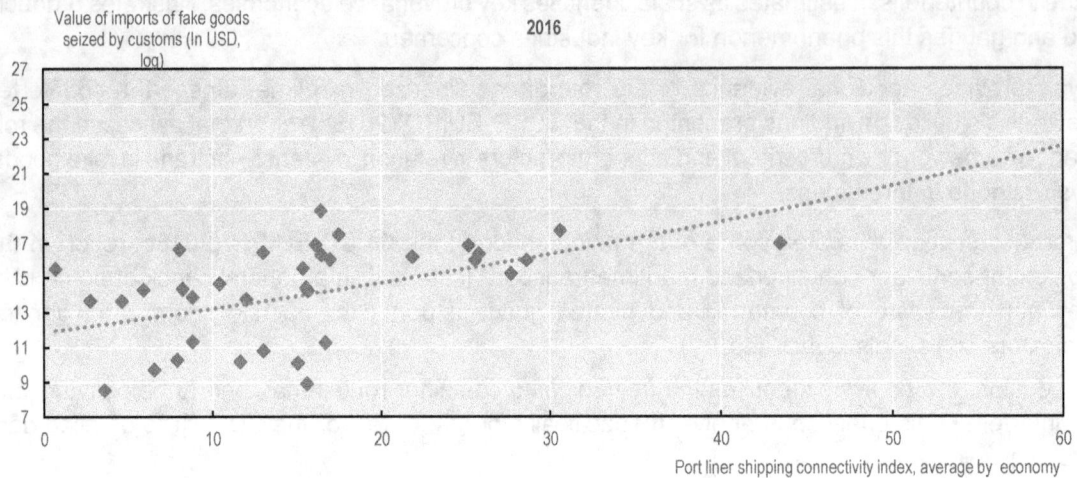

Figure 4.28. Correlation between the Bilateral LSCI index and a proxy for trade in counterfeits. Economy-level, 2016

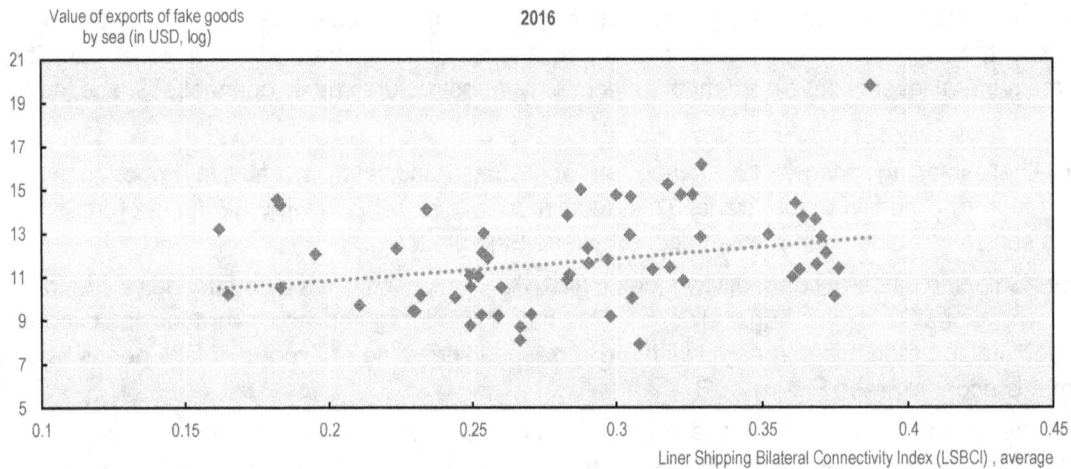

Figure 4.29. Correlation between the Container port traffic index and a proxy for trade in counterfeits. Economy-level, 2016

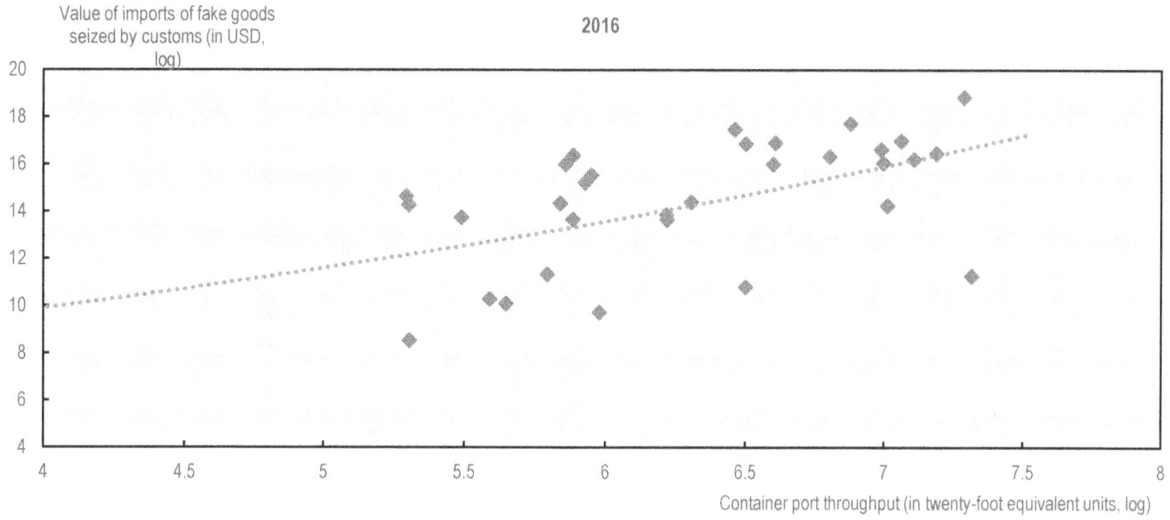

Focus on specific ports (the case of the EU)

The last step of this quantitative exercise identifies the key ports with the highest potential of departure and import of fakes. The available data on seizures, does not permit identification of key ports of entry of fakes. Due to limited data availability, this exercise is done for trade in fakes to the European Union only, and it looks at the flows of legitimate trade in containerships coming from provenance economies with higher GTRIC-e score. As shown in the previous section, the bilateral flows of counterfeit goods, follow by and large the flows of legitimate goods. Consequently, this exercise uses the overall trade flows, and the GTRIC-e scores as a proxy, and relies on an assumpion that criminals do not target specific ports in any particular way. This exercise is done in two steps.

The first step checks which harbours in provenance countries are most likely to be misused as points of departure of trade in fakes to the EU. It has been prepared by comparing seizure data with data on container lines from Comext (Eurostat). For economies with the highest GTRIC-e, we identify ports with the highest number of container ships departing to the EU in 2016.

The second step relies on the Eurostat data on volume of containers transported from the five major provenance countries of counterfeit goods and analyses main countries and ports of entry of containers from the provenance countries. The Annex contains more detailed statistics, which focus on the countries and ports of entry of containers from each of the five major provenance countries.

The results of the first exercise are presented in Table 4.2. The analysis suggests that in China, the ports of Shanghai, Ningbo and Qingdao are the key points of departures of fakes via containerships on their way to the EU. Other significant ports include Hong-Kong (China), some ports in the Gulf area, such as Shuiaba in Kuwait, and Jebel Ali in the United Arab Emirates, Sihanoukville in Cambodia and Bar in Montenegro.

Table 4.2. Main ports of exportation of fakes from provenance economies (2016)

Main provenance economies of fake goods shipped to the EU by sea	GTRIC-e	Main ports
China (People's Republic of)	1	China, Shanghai
		China, Ningbo
		China, Qingdao
		China, Yantian
		China, Xiamen
		China, Xingang
		China, Dalian
		China, Shekou
Hong Kong (China)	1	Hong Kong (China)
Kuwait	1	Kuwait, Shuaiba
		Kuwait, Shuwaikh
Cambodia	0.9673012	Cambodia, Sihanoukville
Montenegro	0.9492664	Montenegro, Bar
United Arab Emirates	0.9453318	United Arab Emirates, Jebel Ali
		United Arab Emirates, Khor Fakkan
		United Arab Emirates, Khalifa
Benin	0.9254637	Benin, Cotonou
Jordan	0.8705141	Jordan, Aqaba
Singapore	0.8620592	Singapore, Singapore
Malaysia	0.8414308	Malaysia, Port Klang
		Malaysia, Tanjung Pelepas
		Malaysia, Pasir Gudang
		Malaysia, Penang
Viet Nam	0.8394201	Viet Nam, Ho Chi Minh City
		Viet Nam, Vung Tau
		Viet Nam, Haiphong
Lebanon	0.8132287	Lebanon, Beirut
Syrian Arab Republic	0.7897374	Syrian Arab Republic, Latakia
		Syrian Arab Republic, Tartous
Morocco	0.7464321	Morocco, Tanger Med
		Morocco, Casablanca
		Morocco, Agadir
Bangladesh	0.7143928	Bangladesh, Chittagong
		Bangladesh, Mongla

The results of the second exercise, summarized in Table 4.3, show that over half of containers transported in 2016 by ships from major counterfeits provenance countries entered the EU through Germany, Netherlands and the United Kingdom. The share of containers transported from major counterfeit provenance economies is also relatively higher for those countries than their share in overall volume of containers transported to the EU. There are also some countries, with relatively low volume of containers handled but with high share of containers transported from major provenance of counterfeit, such as Bulgaria, Romania, Croatia and Greece.

Table 4.3. Main countries of entry of containers in maritime transport from the five major counterfeit provenance countries (2016)

Country	Volume	Share in total volume handled by country	Share of country in total volume of containers handled in the EU	Sensitivity indicator
Germany	2286529	29.85%	19.65%	1.25
Netherlands	2015595	30.54%	17.32%	1.28
United Kingdom	1887239	36.63%	16.22%	1.54
Spain	1504585	19.82%	12.93%	0.83
Belgium	836775	16.98%	7.19%	0.71
Greece	794380	35.92%	6.83%	1.51
France	791238	31.12%	6.80%	1.31
Italy	716195	12.86%	6.15%	0.54
Portugal	182190	12.74%	1.57%	0.54
Poland	180257	16.17%	1.55%	0.68
Romania	153097	43.46%	1.32%	1.82
Sweden	72852	9.33%	0.63%	0.39
Bulgaria	64214	61.78%	0.55%	2.59
Slovenia	53033	11.90%	0.46%	0.50
Croatia	41901	39.64%	0.36%	1.66
Denmark	38881	10.25%	0.33%	0.43
Malta	11998	20.69%	0.10%	0.87
Cyprus*	3976	2.17%	0.03%	0.09
Ireland	1834	0.40%	0.02%	0.02

Notes: Data source: Eurostat table mar_go_qm_c2016 Volume of containers transported to/from main ports. Table 4.31 presents inward flow of total number of containers (loaded and empty) from five major counterfeit provenance countries: China, Hong Kong (China), Singapore, United Arab Emirates and Turkey. For the table quarterly data has been aggregated to annual figures.
Countries not present in the table either not receive the containers via maritime transport or did not provide data.

* Note by Turkey:
The information in this document with reference to "Cyprus" relates to the southern part of the Island. There is no single authority representing both Turkish and Greek Cypriot people on the Island. Turkey recognises the Turkish Republic of Northern Cyprus (TRNC). Until a lasting and equitable solution is found within the context of the United Nations, Turkey shall preserve its position concerning the "Cyprus issue".
Note by all the European Union Member States of the OECD and the European Union:
The Republic of Cyprus is recognised by all members of the United Nations with the exception of Turkey. The information in this document relates to the area under the effective control of the Government of the Republic of Cyprus.

Slightly over 50% of all the containers transported from five major provenance countries of counterfeits by maritime transport to Europe entered in 2016 through four ports: Rotterdam, Hamburg, Felixstowe and Antwerp. Among those ports only for Antwerp, the share of port in the inward transport of containers from five major countries of counterfeit provenance is lower than its share in the overall transport of containers. The importance of containers shipped from major counterfeit provenance countries was especially high for Felixstowe, where shipments from those countries constituted almost 60% of all the containers handled in the port.

Table 4.4. Main ports of entry of containers from the five major counterfeit provenance countries (2016)

Port	Country	Volume	Share in total volume handled by port	Share of port in total volume of containers handled in the EU	Sensitivity indicator
Rotterdam	NL	2015595	31.51%	17.32%	1.32
Hamburg	DE	1837346	39.71%	15.79%	1.67
Felixstowe	UK	1196927	58.92%	10.29%	2.47
Antwerp	BE	821229	17.00%	7.06%	0.71
Peiraias	EL	780582	41.03%	6.71%	1.72
Valencia	ES	739046	31.28%	6.35%	1.31
Southampton	UK	511145	49.87%	4.39%	2.09
Bremerhaven	DE	448718	17.07%	3.86%	0.72
Le Havre	FR	416492	33.15%	3.58%	1.39
Barcelona	ES	340787	30.46%	2.93%	1.28
Algeciras	ES	340283	14.25%	2.92%	0.60
Marseille	FR	322081	51.76%	2.77%	2.17
La Spezia	IT	227881	32.75%	1.96%	1.38
Gdansk	PL	180257	23.33%	1.55%	0.98
Sines	PT	177820	23.54%	1.53%	0.99
Constanta	RO	153097	43.46%	1.32%	1.82
Trieste	IT	150768	47.29%	1.30%	1.99
Gioia Tauro	IT	142086	7.20%	1.22%	0.30
London	UK	129177	17.08%	1.11%	0.72
Genova	IT	109459	9.5%	0.94%	0.40

Notes: Data source: Eurostat table mar_go_qm_c2016 Volume of containers transported to/from main ports. Tables 4.31 and 4.32 presents inward flow of total number of containers (loaded and empty) from five major counterfeit provenance countries: China, Hong Kong (China), Singapore, United Arab Emirates and Turkey. For the table quarterly data has been aggregated to annual figures.
Sensitivity indicator has been computed by dividing share of a country/port in inward transport of containers from five major counterfeit provenance economy by the share of a country/port in overall inward transport of containers.

The Belt and Road Initiative

To complete the existing picture, it is important to highlight that on-going and planned infrastructure developments can change significantly the patterns of imports on fake goods with containers. The Chinese Belt and Road Initiative (BRI; see Box 4.2) seems to be of particular relevance, as a global initiative, that also aims to strengthen container trade connection with the European Union and may facilitate illicit trade.[18]

> **Box 4.2. Belt and Road Initiative (BRI)**
>
> China's Belt and Road Initiative (BRI) development strategy aims to build connectivity and co-operation across six main economic corridors encompassing China and i) Mongolia and Russia, ii) Eurasian countries, iii) Central and West Asia, iv) Pakistan, v) other countries of the Indian sub-continent, and vi) Indochina. The focus of the BRI is to carry out large infrastructural investment projects to facilitate trade and investment.
>
> BRI investment projects are estimated to add over USD 1 trillion of outward funding for foreign infrastructure over the 10-year period from 2017. The main sources of funding for the bulk of these BRI-participating projects are the Chinese development banks, the USD 40 billion Silk Road Fund, and two of the large state-owned commercial banks.
>
> In China, the initiative is overseen by the "Leading Group" for promoting its work hosted by the National Development and Reform Commission (NDRC) which oversees and coordinates all BRI projects (including inter alia with the Ministry of Commerce (MOFCOM), the Ministry of Foreign Affairs (MFA), and the Development Research Centre of the State Council.
>
> Source: OECD (2018).

As demonstrated in the OECD-EUIPO (2018c) report, investments in infrastructure development is one of the key elements that can spur illicit trade, when they are not complemented with sufficient development in governance frameworks. Infrastructure-related factors that can support trade in general and can increase trade in fakes, including i) low shipping charges, ii) fast, simple and predictable customs formalities, and iii) good quality trade and transport-related infrastructure (e.g. ports, railroads, roads and information technology) are factors that tend to be misused by criminals, especially in economies with underdeveloped governance standards, and relevant capacities to implement these standards.

Over time, China has managed to reduce its dependence upon external transit hubs, to increase the internal connectivity of its own port system, and to strengthen its dominance towards an increasing number of foreign nodes and trade partners through the maritime network (Ducruet and Liehui, 2018). The large infrastructure investments along the Belt and Road Initiative will certainly further the changes in container ship transport patterns, and will impact the routes of trade in fake goods.

The BRI will strengthen container trade connection from China to the European Union. The plans include a set of large infrastructure investments designed to go from China's coast to Europe through the South China Sea and the Indian Ocean. Through this connection, China will significantly strengthen the container shipping capacities with the Persian Gulf and the Mediterranean Sea through Central Asia and the Indian Ocean. Several economic studies, based on trade modelling, highlight that BRI-related enhancement in infrastructure in South East Europe are likely to result in significant growths in cargo transhipped in Mediterranean ports (Schinas and von Westarp, 2017; Jiang, Li and Gong, 2018). In fact, Mediterranean Basin plays a central role in the BRI network as a "hub-of-hubs" (Haralambides and Merk, 2020).

Over the recent years China has significantly increased its investment in the foreign port infrastructure. Since 2013, the year of BRI adoption, China has participated in construction and operation of 42 ports in 34 economies (Haralambides and Merk, 2020). Port infrastructure developments are in some cases combined with the creation of Free Trade Zones. Some of the most prominent Chinese investments in the port infrastructure are listed in Table 4.5 and

Table 4.6. Those investments are often backed by the Chinese government and financed from state loans, which allows the Chinese companies to offer better deal terms than those possible for the major competitors. The rapid growth of port of Piraeus[19] illustrates well the ability of Chinese port operators to drive the maritime traffic to the ports they control.

Chinese investments in the crucial port infrastructure abroad may be driven by many legitimate strategic and commercial goals, but also raises some security and safety concern for host countries. One of them is a shift in port operators' incentives towards major emphasis on trade facilitation and reduction of transport time in lieu of more thorough control of containers. Such a shift renders counterfeit detection more difficult and less efficient.

This might result in substantial growth of fakes entering the European Union in container ships. Current analysis points at ports in northern Europe as the main ports of entry of fake. After completion of these investments, and in line with findings of OECD (2018c), ports in the Mediterranean region could become more intensely targeted by criminal networks in the context of smuggling fakes to the European Union.

In addition, the presence of free trade zones (FTZs) is a particularly strong driver of trade in counterfeit and pirated goods in economies with weak governance, high corruption levels and a lack of intellectual property rights (IPR) enforcement (OECD/EUIPO, 2018a). In the context of the BRI initiative, there are strong intentions to create new FTZs along the Silk Road. As outlined in the Chinese Five-Year plan (Chapter 52 Section 2): *We will speed up efforts to implement the free trade area strategy, gradually establishing a network of high-standard free trade areas. We will actively engage in negotiations with countries and regions along the routes of the Belt and Road Initiative on the building of free trade areas.*

Table 4.5. Selected acquisitions of port operation undertakings by Chinese firms in Europe

Year	Port	Terminal	Company	Majority Stake?
2004	Antwerp	Port of Antwerp Gateway Terminal	COSCO Shipping Ports Limited	No
2009	Piraeus	Container Terminals 2# and 3#	COSCO Shipping Ports Limited	Yes
2013	Antwerp	Antwerp Gateway[1]	China Merchants Port Holdings Company Limited	No
2013	Dunkirk	Terminal des Flandres[1]	China Merchants Port Holdings Company Limited	No
2013	Le Havre	Terminal de France and Terminal Nord[1]	China Merchants Port Holdings Company Limited	No
2013	Montoir	Terminal du Grand Ouest[1]	China Merchants Port Holdings Company Limited	No
2013	Fos	Eurofos[1]	China Merchants Port Holdings Company Limited	No
2013	Marsaxlokk	Malta Freeport Terminal[1]	China Merchants Port Holdings Company Limited	No
2015	Kumport	Kumport Terminal	COSCO Shipping Ports Limited	Yes
2015	Kumport	Kumport Terminal	China Merchants Port Holdings Company Limited	Yes
2016	Vado	existing Reefer Terminal S.P.A and the new terminal under construction	COSCO Shipping Ports Limited	No
2016	Rotterdam	Euromax Terminal	COSCO Shipping Ports Limited	No
2016	Piraeus	Piraeus Port Authority	COSCO Shipping Ports Limited	Yes
2017	Zeebrugge	APM/CSP Terminal Zeebrugge	COSCO Shipping Ports Limited	Yes
2017	Valencia	Noatum Container Terminal Valencia[2]	COSCO Shipping Ports Limited	Yes
2017	Bilbao	Noatum Container Terminal Bilbao[2]	COSCO Shipping Ports Limited	Yes
2018	Thessaloniki	Thessaloniki Port Authority	China Merchants Port Holdings Company Limited	No
2020	Odessa	Odessa Terminal Holdco Ltd[3]	China Merchants Port Holdings Company Limited	No
2020	Rotterdam	Rotterdam World Gateway[3]	China Merchants Port Holdings Company Limited	No

Notes: 1 Through purchase of 49% of stakes in Terminal Link company. 2 Through takeover of Noatum Ports. 3 Through Terminal Link company.
Sources: Chen, Jihong & Fei, Yijie & Lee, Paul & Tao, Xuezong. (2018). Overseas Port Investment Policy for China's Central and Local Governments in the Belt and Road Initiative. Journal of Contemporary China. 28. 1-20.; Annual reports of companies, press releases and press articles.

Table 4.6. Selected acquisitions of port operation undertakings by Chinese firms in Asia

Year	Port	Terminal	Company	Majority Stake?
2003	Singapore	Pasir Panjang Terminal 1	COSCO Shipping Ports Limited	No
2010	Vung Tau	Vung Tau Container Terminal	China Merchants Port Holdings Company Limited	No
2011	Colombo	South Container Terminal of Colombo Port	China Merchants Port Holdings Company Limited	Yes
2012	Kaohsiung	Taiwan Kao Ming Container Terminal	COSCO Shipping Ports Limited	No
2013	Busan	Busan New Container Terminal[1]	China Merchants Port Holdings Company Limited	No
2013	Gwadar	Gwadar Deep-water	China Overseas Ports Holding Company Pakistan (Pvt.) Ltd.	Yes
2015	Busan	Busan	COSCO Shipping Ports Limited	No
2015	Haifa	Haifa Bayport	Shanghai International Port Group	Yes
2015	Kuantan	Kuantan	Guangxi Beibu Gulf International Port Group	No
2016	Abu Dhabi	CSP Abu Dhabi Terminal	COSCO Shipping Ports Limited	Yes
2016	Singapore	Pasir Panjang Terminal 5	COSCO Shipping Ports Limited	No
2017	Hambantota	Hambantota International Port Group	China Merchants Port Holdings Company Limited	Yes
2020	Singapore	CMA CGM-PSA Lion Terminal Pte Ltd[2]	China Merchants Port Holdings Company Limited	No
2020	Laem Chabang	Laem Chabang International Terminal Co Ltd[2]	China Merchants Port Holdings Company Limited	No
2020	Umm Qasr	CMA CGM Terminals Iraq S.A.S.[2]	China Merchants Port Holdings Company Limited	No

Notes: 1 Through purchase of 49% of stakes in Terminal Link company. 2 Through Terminal Link company
Sources: Chen, Jihong & Fei, Yijie & Lee, Paul & Tao, Xuezong. (2018). Overseas Port Investment Policy for China's Central and Local Governments in the Belt and Road Initiative. Journal of Contemporary China. 28. 1-20.; Annual reports of companies, press releases and press articles.

Table 4.7. Selected acquisition of port operation undertakings by Chinese firms in other regions

Year	Port	Terminal	Company	Majority Stake?
		North America		
2001	Long Beach	Pacific Container Terminal	COSCO Shipping Ports Limited	Yes
2002	Los Angeles	West Basin Container Terminal	COSCO Shipping Ports Limited	Yes
2008	Seattle	SSA Terminals	COSCO Shipping Ports Limited	No
2013	Houston	Houston Terminal Link[1]	China Merchants Port Holdings Company Limited	No
2013	Miami	South Florida Container Terminal[1]	China Merchants Port Holdings Company Limited	No
2020	Kingston	Kingston Freeport Terminal Limited[2]	China Merchants Port Holdings Company Limited	No
		South America		
2017	Paranaguá	Terminal de Contêineres de Paranaguá	China Merchants Port Holdings Company Limited	Yes
2019	Chancay	Chancay Terminal	COSCO Shipping Ports Limited	Yes
		Africa		
2007	Said	Said	COSCO Shipping Ports Limited	No
2010	Lagos	Tin-Can Island Container Terminal	China Merchants Port Holdings Company Limited	No
2012	Lomé	Togo Container Terminal	China Merchants Port Holdings Company Limited	Yes
2013	Djibouti	Doraleh Container Terminal	China Merchants Port Holdings Company Limited	No
2013	Casablanca	Somaport[1]	China Merchants Port Holdings Company Limited	No
2013	Tangiers	Eurogate Tanger[1]	China Merchants Port Holdings Company Limited	No
2013	Abidjan	Terra Abidjan[1]	China Merchants Port Holdings Company Limited	No
		Oceania		
2018	Newcastle	Newcastle	China Merchants Port Holdings Company Limited	Yes

Notes: 1 Through purchase of 49% of stakes in Terminal Link company. 2 Through Terminal Link company.
Sources: Chen, Jihong & Fei, Yijie & Lee, Paul & Tao, Xuezong. (2018). Overseas Port Investment Policy for China's Central and Local Governments in the Belt and Road Initiative. Journal of Contemporary China. 28. 1-20.; Annual reports of companies, press releases and press articles.

References

Chen, J. et al. (2018), Overseas Port Investment Policy for China's Central and Local Governments in the Belt and Road Initiative. Journal of Contemporary China. 28. 1-20. 10.1080/10670564.2018.1511392.

Comext (2020), "DS-022469 - EXTRA EU Trade Since 1999 By Mode of Transport (NSTR)", Eurostat International Trade Statistics (database), http://epp.eurostat.ec.europa.eu/newxtweb/setupdimselection.do, (last access on February 2020).

Ducruet C. and L. Wang (2018), China's Global Shipping Connectivity: Internal and External Dynamics in the Contemporary Era (1890–2016). Chinese Geographical Science, 28(2): 202–216. https://doi.org/10.1007/s11769-018-0942-x.

Haralambides, H., Merk, O (2020) The Belt and Road Initiative: Impacts on Global Maritime Trade Flows. International Transport Forum, Discussion Paper 178.

ITF (2020a), "Global Container Shipping and the Coronavirus", COVID-19 Transport Brief, International Transport Forum, OECD, https://www.itf-oecd.org/sites/default/files/global-container-shipping-covid-19.pdf.

Jiang, B., J. Li, C. Gong (2018), Maritime Shipping and Export Trade on "Maritime Silk Road", The Asian Journal of Shipping and Logistics 34(2) (2018) 083-090.

OECD (2008), The Economic Impact of Counterfeiting and Piracy, OECD Publishing, Paris, https://doi.org/10.1787/9789264045521-en.

OECD/EUIPO (2019), *Trends in Trade in Counterfeit and Pirated Goods*, Illicit Trade, OECD Publishing, Paris, https://doi.org/10.1787/g2g9f533-en.

OECD/EUIPO (2018a), Trade in Counterfeit Goods and Free Trade Zones: Evidence from Recent Trends, OECD Publishing, Paris, http://dx.doi.org/10.1787/9789264289550-en.

OECD/EUIPO (2018b), *Misuse of Small Parcels for Trade in Counterfeit Goods: Facts and Trends*, OECD Publishing, Paris, https://doi.org/10.1787/9789264307858-en.

OECD/EUIPO (2018c), *Why Do Countries Export Fakes?*, OECD Publishing, Paris, https://doi.org/10.1787/9789264302464-en.

OECD (2018) "China's Belt and Road Initiative in the Global Trade, Investment and Finance Landscape", Chapter 2 of the OECD Business and Financial Outlook, OECD, Paris.

OECD/EUIPO (2017), *Mapping the Real Routes of Trade in Fake Goods*, OECD Publishing, Paris, http://dx.doi.org/10.1787/9789264278349-en.

Schinas O. and A. Graf von Westarp (2017), "Assessing the impact of the maritime silk road": Journal of Ocean Engineering and Science, Volume 2, Issue 3, September 2017, pp. 186-195.

5 Conclusions and areas for action

Over time, containers have brought numerous benefits to businesses, providing them with efficient and affordable ways of trading of all kinds of goods globally. Importantly, the great flexibility and multimodality of containers have further enhanced trade, providing flexible solutions at relatively low-cost. Today, despite the COVID-19 crisis, containerised maritime trade continues to thrive as the key enabler of globalization.

Trade facilitation initiatives taken by international organisations such as the WCO and the WTO have provided additional impetus to the trade expansion, to the advantage of businesses of all sizes. The recent expansion of free trade zones as intermediate points of trade and centres of economic activity has also been crucial, offering suitable solutions to handle goods in transit.

On the other hand, trade facilitation made it easier in many ways for organised crime and other criminal actors to pursue lucrative illicit activities, including the movement of prohibited goods across borders. Misuse of containerized maritime transport for illicit trade in tobacco, wildlife and counterfeit products have flourished. In fact, counterfeits trafficked by container ships clearly dominate in terms of value.

The attractiveness of containerized maritime transport for counterfeiters has increased over time, benefitting from the advances in interoperability of containers, the anonymity of containers, the growing complexity of trade routes, alliances and vessel sharing agreements, and the fragmented governance structure of maritime transport that facilitates diffusion of responsibility of the private sector for illicit maritime trade. Even though the losses on confiscated cargoes could be large, the risk of detection may be low in ocean freight given the rapid growth in volume of freight and the progressively growing complexity of routes.

The quantitative analysis in this report provides evidence of the scale and magnitude of misuse of containerized maritime transport. This analysis is based primarily on data on customs seizures of counterfeit goods obtained from the World Customs Organization, European Commission's Directorate-General for Taxation and Customs Union and from the US Customs and Border Protection (CBP).

The analysis shows that, fakes shipped in containers clearly dominate in terms of value of seized goods and the number of items. Only in terms of number of seizures, small parcels are on top. Between 2014 and 2016, an average of almost 56% of the value of customs seizures of IP-infringing goods worldwide concerned sea shipments.

The highest number of counterfeits shipped with containers originated in East Asia, with China and Hong Kong (China) at the top of the ranking, followed by India, Malaysia, Mexico, Singapore, Thailand, Turkey and the United Arab Emirates. Hong-Kong (China); Singapore and The United Arab Emirates are important transit points in illicit containerized trade in counterfeits.

Regarding the industry-specific patterns, container ships tend to be universally misused by counterfeiters in virtually all the sectors analysed. In product categories where counterfeiting is a particularly big problem, containers are more intensely used. This is the case for perfumes and cosmetics, foodstuff, footwear and toys and games, where more than 70% of seizures of counterfeits concerned sea shipments.

Illicit trade in counterfeits that misuses maritime transport is a universal and general problem, which should be a concern to all shipping lines that use containers. Put differently, counterfeiters have used all container lines, as they become an attractive way of smuggling counterfeit goods that offer high rewards and low risks. These challenges posed by the large volumes of fakes in containers have been significant for customs authorities responsible for handling containers as they cross borders, and much attention has been paid internationally, at the WCO and elsewhere. The information that has been traditionally available, for example through ship manifests, and the supporting role of customs brokers are often absent in small volume trade. The information has generally been provided in paper form; it has thus not been available electronically and, it is susceptible to forging.

In addition, customs resources are limited, and their responsibilities cover many areas, counterfeits being just one of them. This has created a dilemma for customs, as they have had to balance the need for expedited processing of imports, with the need for properly assessing duties and monitoring imports with a view towards countering counterfeit and other illicit trade. A close review of imports would necessarily cause delays that would not be acceptable, and, given the difficulty in identifying counterfeit items, it would not be cost-effective. The volume of container trade further complicates the situation, given that on a single ship there can be many thousands of containers.

Next steps

The magnitude and scope of the problem have captured the attention of governments and many initiatives have been taken to combat illicit trade. Although progress has been made, criminal elements have been quick to adapt to changing circumstances, finding new ways to elude detection and restriction of their illegal activities. In addition, the recent COVID crisis has re-shaped this already complex situation by suddenly changing the existing trade routes and re-defining enforcement priorities.

Risk assessment has been an important tool for customs in combatting illicit trade in counterfeits in maritime transport, but physical checks have been the most effective method of interception. Given the very high labour intensity of these checks there is a considerable scope for improving risk assessment techniques, and improving the quantity and reliability of information. Seaports should up their game and improve their capability for effective scrutiny of cargo. Several ports have created Wildlife Traffic Monitoring Units to detect and prevent the illegal transport of wildlife. Application of modern technologies with a view towards the use of electronic manifests would facilitate risk assessment, which relies critically on data quality and detailed information to be successful.

In addition, some efforts are being made by the industry to enhance co-ordination in efforts to counter the threat of illicit trade in maritime transport. These efforts manifest in several ways. For example, the progress in standard setting that in fact enabled the emergence of modern containers indicates a potential path for further efforts. Another example is the declaration of intent, in which well-known brand owners, vessels operators, and freight forwarders worked together to develop a voluntary guidelines, which aim to raise awareness of the importance of gathering sufficient information on the parties using shipping services. It appears that there is considerable scope for improvement in this regard, as there are, among other things, privacy issues to be addressed, along with confidentiality concerns.

Maritime transport companies, for their part, could use their pivotal role in supply chains to better scrutinise their cargo. Commitments to move cargo only for clients that comply with certification schemes, such as those aimed at protecting natural forests would go a long way. These are common in palm oil, timber and paper supply chains, but rarer in the soy and cattle sectors. These schemes could inspire similar initiatives to counter illicit trade in counterfeits misusing containerized maritime transport.

Last, it should be noted that the recent COVID crisis presents a significant challenge, but also an opportunity to further policy discussions in this area. The crisis is a challenge, as it introduces much volatility in the markets, changes trade routes and reshapes priorities of enforcement efforts. At the same time, it is also an opportunity, since it puts increased attention on illicit trade and enforcement, and hence opens a window of possibility for significant progress to be made.

Annex A.

Table A A.1. Main countries of entry of containers in maritime transport from China (2016)

Country	Volume	UNCTAD connectivity index	Share in total volume handled by country	Share of country in total volume of containers handled in the EU	Sensitivity indicator
Germany	1815235	0.73	23.70%	22.73%	1.45
Netherlands	1583418	0.71	23.99%	19.82%	1.47
United Kingdom	1385366	0.72	26.89%	17.34%	1.64
Spain	950031	0.72	12.51%	11.89%	0.77
France	577633	0.71	22.72%	7.23%	1.39
Belgium	438217	0.73	8.89%	5.49%	0.54
Greece	426631	0.53	19.29%	5.34%	1.18
Italy	329098	0.66	5.91%	4.12%	0.36
Poland	179085	0.52	16.06%	2.24%	0.98
Portugal	99156	0.52	6.93%	1.24%	0.42
Sweden	43166	0.50	5.53%	0.54%	0.34
Romania	43108	0.40	12.24%	0.54%	0.75
Slovenia	40125	0.43	9.01%	0.50%	0.55
Denmark	38269	0.48	10.09%	0.48%	0.62
Croatia	28545	0.43	27.01%	0.36%	1.65
Malta	6689	0.57	11.54%	0.08%	0.71
Cyprus*	3714	0.32	2.03%	0.05%	0.12
Bulgaria	188	0.24	0.18%	0.00%	0.01

Table A A.2. Main ports of entry of containers in maritime transport from China (2016)

Port	Country	Volume	Share in total volume handled by port	Share of port in total volume of containers handled in the EU	Sensitivity indicator
Rotterdam	NL	1583418	24.75%	19.82%	1.51
Hamburg	DE	1450436	31.35%	18.16%	1.92
Felixstowe	UK	866060	42.63%	10.84%	2.61
Peiraias	EL	426631	22.42%	5.34%	1.37
Antwerpen	BE	423034	8.76%	5.30%	0.54
Valencia	ES	402945	17.05%	5.04%	1.04
Southampton	UK	380051	37.08%	4.76%	2.27
Bremerhaven	DE	364797	13.87%	4.57%	0.85
Le Havre	FR	324911	25.86%	4.07%	1.58
Barcelona	ES	273715	24.46%	3.43%	1.50
Algeciras	ES	217002	9.09%	2.72%	0.56
Marseille	FR	210957	33.90%	2.64%	2.07
La Spezia	IT	188769	27.13%	2.36%	1.66

Gdansk	PL	179085	23.18%	2.24%	1.42
London	UK	110329	14.59%	1.38%	0.89
Sines	PT	98570	13.05%	1.23%	0.80
Genova	IT	70742	6.18%	0.89%	0.38
Göteborg	SE	43162	10.55%	0.54%	0.65
Constanta	RO	43108	12.24%	0.54%	0.75
Koper	SI	40125	9.01%	0.50%	0.55

Table A A.3. Main countries of entry of containers in maritime transport from Turkey (2016)

Country	Volume	UNCTAD connectivity index	Share in total volume handled by country	Share of country in total volume of containers handled in the EU	Sensitivity indicator
Spain	340049	0.51	4.48%	17.72%	1.14
Greece	323047	0.51	14.61%	16.83%	3.72
Italy	270053	0.51	4.85%	14.07%	1.23
United Kingdom	264890	0.47	5.14%	13.80%	1.31
Belgium	247617	0.50	5.03%	12.90%	1.28
Romania	109916	0.40	31.20%	5.73%	7.94
France	87139	0.47	3.43%	4.54%	0.87
Portugal	82224	0.40	5.75%	4.28%	1.46
Germany	81580	0.47	1.07%	4.25%	0.27
Bulgaria	64026	0.29	61.60%	3.34%	15.68
Netherlands	35297	0.46	0.53%	1.84%	0.14
Slovenia	6390	0.33	1.43%	0.33%	0.37
Malta	4208	0.41	7.26%	0.22%	1.85
Ireland	1834	0.29	0.40%	0.10%	0.10
Croatia	1048	0.31	0.99%	0.05%	0.25
Sweden	140	0.38	0.02%	0.01%	0.00

Table A A.4. Main ports of entry of containers in maritime transport from Turkey (2016)

Port	Country	Volume	Share in total volume handled by port	Share of port in total volume of containers handled in the EU	Sensitivity indicator
Peiraias	EL	309249	16.25%	16.11%	4.14
Antwerpen	BE	247617	5.13%	12.90%	1.30
Felixstowe	UK	239623	11.80%	12.48%	3.00
Valencia	ES	191313	8.10%	9.97%	2.06
Constanta	RO	109916	31.20%	5.73%	7.94
Trieste	IT	99701	31.28%	5.19%	7.96
Algeciras	ES	92015	3.85%	4.79%	0.98
Gioia Tauro	IT	81046	4.11%	4.22%	1.05
Sines	PT	78531	10.40%	4.09%	2.65
Bremerhaven	DE	51810	1.97%	2.70%	0.50
Le Havre	FR	43442	3.46%	2.26%	0.88
Cagliari	IT	43376	16.32%	2.26%	4.15
Marseille	FR	36040	5.79%	1.88%	1.47
Varna	BG	35476	49.74%	1.85%	12.66
Rotterdam	NL	35297	0.55%	1.84%	0.14

Barcelona	ES	33648	3.01%	1.75%	0.77
La Spezia	IT	29918	4.30%	1.56%	1.09
Hamburg	DE	29322	0.63%	1.53%	0.16
Burgas	BG	28550	87.54%	1.49%	22.28
Liverpool	UK	15558	4.28%	0.81%	1.09

Table A A.5. Main countries of entry of containers in maritime transport from Singapore (2016)

Country	Volume	UNCTAD connectivity index	Share in total volume handled by country	Share of country in total volume of containers handled in the EU	Sensitivity indicator
Netherlands	281621	0.68	4.27%	25.55%	1.89
Germany	233955	0.70	3.05%	21.22%	1.35
United Kingdom	139447	0.70	2.71%	12.65%	1.20
Belgium	129489	0.71	2.63%	11.75%	1.16
Spain	114540	0.65	1.51%	10.39%	0.67
France	84635	0.65	3.33%	7.68%	1.48
Italy	37292	0.65	0.67%	3.38%	0.30
Greece	33953	0.51	1.54%	3.08%	0.68
Sweden	25574	0.50	3.28%	2.32%	1.45
Croatia	12308	0.41	11.65%	1.12%	5.16
Slovenia	6518	0.41	1.46%	0.59%	0.65
Poland	1172	0.52	0.11%	0.11%	0.05
Portugal	650	0.52	0.05%	0.06%	0.02
Denmark	612	0.47	0.16%	0.06%	0.07
Malta	472	0.54	0.81%	0.04%	0.36
Cyprus*	139	0.32	0.08%	0.01%	0.03
Romania	72	0.34	0.02%	0.01%	0.01

Table A A.6. Main ports of entry of containers in maritime transport from Singapore (2016)

Port	Country	Volume	Share in total volume handled by port	Share of port in total volume of containers handled in the EU	Sensitivity indicator
Rotterdam	NL	281621	4.40%	25.55%	1.95
Hamburg	DE	229981	4.97%	20.86%	2.20
Antwerpen	BE	129460	2.68%	11.74%	1.19
Southampton	UK	95351	9.30%	8.65%	4.12
Valencia	ES	86585	3.66%	7.85%	1.62
Marseille	FR	48340	7.77%	4.38%	3.44
Felixstowe	UK	36411	1.79%	3.30%	0.79
Le Havre	FR	35628	2.84%	3.23%	1.26
Peiraias	EL	33953	1.78%	3.08%	0.79
Göteborg	SE	25574	6.25%	2.32%	2.77
Genova	IT	16274	1.42%	1.48%	0.63
Barcelona	ES	15464	1.38%	1.40%	0.61
Rijeka	HR	12308	13.76%	1.12%	6.10
Algeciras	ES	12068	0.51%	1.09%	0.22
Trieste	IT	10967	3.44%	0.99%	1.52
La Spezia	IT	7305	1.05%	0.66%	0.47

London	UK	7167	0.95%	0.65%	0.42
Koper	SI	6518	1.46%	0.59%	0.65
Bremerhaven	DE	3959	0.15%	0.36%	0.07
Cagliari	IT	1307	0.49%	0.12%	0.22

Table A A.7. Main countries of entry of containers in maritime transport from Hong Kong (China) (2016)

Country	Volume	UNCTAD connectivity index	Share in total volume handled by country	Share of country in total volume of containers handled in the EU	Sensitivity indicator
Germany	112162	0.65	1.46%	32.06%	2.04
Netherlands	88979	0.64	1.35%	25.43%	1.88
United Kingdom	77335	0.65	1.50%	22.10%	2.10
France	31327	0.60	1.23%	8.95%	1.72
Spain	17706	0.57	0.23%	5.06%	0.33
Greece	9716	0.49	0.44%	2.78%	0.61
Italy	5396	0.56	0.10%	1.54%	0.14
Sweden	3972	0.45	0.51%	1.14%	0.71
Belgium	2976	0.63	0.06%	0.85%	0.08
Malta	251	0.48	0.43%	0.07%	0.60
Portugal	73	0.49	0.01%	0.02%	0.01
Romania	1	0.32	0.00%	0.00%	0.00

Table A A.8. Main ports of entry of containers in maritime transport from Hong Kong (China) (2016)

Port	Country	Volume	Share in total volume handled by port	Share of port in total volume of containers handled in the EU	Sensitivity indicator
Hamburg	DE	98072	2.12%	28.03%	2.96
Rotterdam	NL	88979	1.39%	25.43%	1.94
Felixstowe	UK	42127	2.07%	12.04%	2.90
Southampton	UK	33349	3.25%	9.53%	4.54
Marseille	FR	22792	3.66%	6.51%	5.12
Bremerhaven	DE	14090	0.54%	4.03%	0.75
Barcelona	ES	10662	0.95%	3.05%	1.33
Peiraias	EL	9716	0.51%	2.78%	0.71
Le Havre	FR	8101	0.64%	2.32%	0.90
Valencia	ES	5472	0.23%	1.56%	0.32
Genova	IT	4895	0.43%	1.40%	0.60
Göteborg	SE	3972	0.97%	1.14%	1.36
Antwerpen	BE	2976	0.06%	0.85%	0.09
London	UK	1576	0.21%	0.45%	0.29
Algeciras	ES	1013	0.04%	0.29%	0.06
Trieste	IT	366	0.11%	0.10%	0.16
Vigo	ES	336	0.37%	0.10%	0.51
Nantes Saint-Nazaire	FR	266	0.29%	0.08%	0.41
Marsaxlokk	MT	251	0.46%	0.07%	0.64
Forth	UK	180	0.14%	0.05%	0.19

Table A A.9. Main countries of entry of containers in maritime transport from United Arab Emirates (2016)

Country	Volume	UNCTAD connectivity index	Share in total volume handled by country	Share of country in total volume of containers handled in the EU	Sensitivity indicator
Spain	82259	0.60	1.08%	29.66%	1.91
Italy	74356	0.58	1.34%	26.81%	2.35
Germany	43597	0.60	0.57%	15.72%	1.00
Netherlands	26280	0.58	0.40%	9.48%	0.70
United Kingdom	20201	0.60	0.39%	7.29%	0.69
Belgium	18476	0.62	0.37%	6.66%	0.66
France	10504	0.59	0.41%	3.79%	0.73
Greece	1033	0.47	0.05%	0.37%	0.08
Malta	378	0.52	0.65%	0.14%	1.15
Cyprus*	123	0.31	0.07%	0.04%	0.12
Portugal	87	0.48	0.01%	0.03%	0.01

Table A A.10. Main ports of entry of containers in maritime transport from United Arab Emirates (2016)

Port	Country	Volume	Share in total volume handled by port	Share of port in total volume of containers handled in the EU	Sensitivity indicator
Gioia Tauro	IT	57125	2.90%	20.60%	5.10
Valencia	ES	52731	2.23%	19.02%	3.93
Hamburg	DE	29535	0.64%	10.65%	1.12
Rotterdam	NL	26280	0.41%	9.48%	0.72
Algeciras	ES	18185	0.76%	6.56%	1.34
Antwerpen	BE	18142	0.38%	6.54%	0.66
Genova	IT	14307	1.25%	5.16%	2.20
Bremerhaven	DE	14062	0.53%	5.07%	0.94
Felixstowe	UK	12706	0.63%	4.58%	1.10
Barcelona	ES	7298	0.65%	2.63%	1.15
London	UK	4895	0.65%	1.77%	1.14
Le Havre	FR	4410	0.35%	1.59%	0.62
Marseille	FR	3952	0.64%	1.43%	1.12
Southampton	UK	2394	0.23%	0.86%	0.41
Port Réunion (ex Pointe-des-Galets) (Réunion)	FR	1986	1.95%	0.72%	3.43
La Spezia	IT	1816	0.26%	0.65%	0.46
Castellón	ES	1628	1.47%	0.59%	2.59
Peiraias	EL	1033	0.05%	0.37%	0.10
Cartagena	ES	880	1.86%	0.32%	3.28
Las Palmas	ES	602	0.13%	0.22%	0.23

Notes

1. Goods that infringe trademarks, copyrights, patents or design rights.

2. See also https://unctad.org/en/pages/PublicationWebflyer.aspx?publicationid=2245

3. As measured by the average of exports and imports,

4. 20 foot (6.10 m) long and eight foot (2.44 m) wide.

5. The Wall Street Journal, June 27, 2019 "Maersk Looks Toward Shore for Growth. Available at: https://www.wsj.com/articles/maersk-ceo-wants-half-its-earnings-to-come-from-inland-logistics-11561580963

6. See https://mariners.coastguard.blog/category/coronavirus-covid-19/.

7. https://www.itf-oecd.org/sites/default/files/global-container-shipping-covid-19.pdf

8. https://www.alphaliner.com

9. https://lloydslist.maritimeintelligence.informa.com/LL1133882/Carriers-summoned-by-China-to-curb-transpacific-markups

10. https://lloydslist.maritimeintelligence.informa.com/LL1133960/US-warns-box-lines-against-transpacific-collusion

11. https://shippingwatch.com/carriers/Container/article12416589.ece

12. A provenance economy is an economy detected and registered by a reporting customs agency as a source of an item that has been intercepted in violation of an IP right, whatever the amount or value concerned.

13. Note that EUIPO works now with the European Union enforcement authorities to establish best practices in data collection across the EU. The Anti-Counterfeiting Intelligence Support Tool (ACIST) converts the collected data into harmonised format so that it can be compared and aggregated.

14. There are two principles for reporting the value of counterfeit and pirated goods: 1) declared value (value indicated on customs declarations), which corresponds to values reported in the general trade statistics; and 2) replacement value (price of original goods). The structured interviews with customs officials and the descriptive analysis of values of selected products conducted in OECD-EUIPO (2016) revealed that the declared values are reported in most cases.

15. Those are defined in OECD/EUIPO (2017).

16   Formally, the numerator includes the percentage of seizures in container ships in total seizures from a given provenance economy. The denominator includes the average percentage of seizures in container ships across the top 20 provenance economies.

17   For more details on the methodology, see OECD-EUIPO (2017)

[18] The following EU countries are included in the BRI: Bulgaria, Croatia, Czech Republic, Estonia, Hungary, Latvia, Lithuania, Poland, Romania, Slovakia, Slovenia, Other countries from the region included in the BRI are: Albania, Armenia, Azerbaijan, Belarus, Bosnia and Herzegovina, Georgia, Former Yugoslav Republic of Macedonia, Moldova, Montenegro, Russian Federation, Serbia, Turkey and Ukraine.

[19] Between 1st quarter of 2010 and 1st quarter of 2020 the rank of Piraeus in UNCTAD Port liner shipping connectivity index rose from position 62 to 27 among almost 1300 ports ranked in the index. Port of Piraeus increased the volume of containers handled over the period of 2010 and 2019 more than six times and its share in total volume of containers handled in European ports from 1.3% to over 6% in the same period.

www.ingramcontent.com/pod-product-compliance
Lightning Source LLC
LaVergne TN
LVHW061947070526
838199LV00060B/4008